DENIS COMPTON

Norman Giller

André Deutsch

First published in Great Britain in 1997 by André Deutsch Limited
106 Great Russell Street, London WC1B 3LJ.

André Deutsch is a subsidiary of VCI plc.

A catalogue record for this title is available from the British Library

ISBN 0 233 99259 6

Printed in Finland by WSOY

Contents

*This book is dedicated
to the memories of
DCSC and WJE.
They ran together
into the record books
and into our hearts*

Opening Spell

By Norman Giller

THE television cameras and studio microphones had just been switched off, and Denis Compton stood cuddling the famous red *This Is Your Life* book that had minutes earlier been presented to him by programme host Eamonn Andrews. Alongside Compo beamed his old sparring partner and pal Keith Miller, who had been flown in as a surprise guest from Australia. "Just think, Nugget," Denis whispered mischievously to Keith, "the stories they *could* have told...!"

The eyes of the two sixty-something sporting idols suddenly twinkled like cut diamonds as a hundred recollections queued for a place in their memories.

I was a privileged witness to this confidential moment in my role as scriptwriter for the show, an assignment I would willingly have paid to carry out after decades of hero-worship and then friendship with The Great Entertainer.

"What a book it would make," I said to Denis. "*The Untold Stories.*"

"Not a chance, old boy," he replied. "It would need to be printed on asbestos!"

Well, that only made me more determined to write a fireproof book about one of the truly outstanding sporting folk heroes of the century.

I have researched the book on and off for the little matter of forty-two years! When I was a young sportsroom assistant

1

at the much mourned London *Evening News* in 1955 I was seconded to do the background research for a secret pull-out supplement headlined:FAREWELL COMPO. The *News* cricket correspondent, E.M. Wellings, had been tipped off that Denis would never play again following an operation to remove his right kneecap. We were about to go to press when a statement was released from the surgeon that Denis *would* play again. The headline was hastily changed to WELCOME BACK COMPO!

Little did I know it then, but I had laid the foundation to this book with dozens of quotes and anecdotes from all manner of people in Compo's life, including his parents, schoolteachers and early Middlesex team-mates.

Along with thousands of other star-struck schoolboys from my generation, I queued in the early postwar years to watch Compton's centuries and to chase his autograph. His goals for Arsenal and dribbling left-wing runs for the wartime England team were another source of wonder.

The calendar moves forward to 1964, when I joined the same Express Newspapers staff as Denis. I am always wary of getting in touching distance of a sporting hero, but over the next ten years of working in the same Fleet Street office (I was for some time chief football reporter on the *Daily Express*) this was an idol who grew rather than diminished in my estimation. He was everything you hope for in a hero: entertaining, modest and always approachable.

"I'll have a large G and T, old boy," was the opening line to many fascinating conversations about his incredible life and times. Keith Miller, his greatest friend and rival from Down Under, was also on the *Express* staff, and my sportsroom colleagues and I used to have wonderful sessions in Fleet Street watering holes such as El Vinos and the Cheshire Cheese listening to them swapping summertime yarns about their Test battles and off-the-pitch escapades.

Forward now to 1987, and by this time I was a scriptwriter

for *This Is Your Life*. Eamonn Andrews told me when we decided to make Denis the subject, "I am going to put two researchers on the programme who don't know a leg before from a leg over. I do not want this to be a sports documentary, but just to make sure we cover the best cricket and football stories I want you to get Denis talking his head off."

Eamonn then added with as stern a look as he could create on that friendly Irish face, "Don't, whatever you do, give him the tiniest hint that I am after him with the Big Red Book."

True to his word, Eamonn appointed Sue Green, now the show's producer, as main researcher. By her own admission, Sue does not know one end of a cricket bat from the other, but she got on famously with Denis's wife, Christine, in their clandestine meetings and she expertly dug out the salient family background facts. Assigned to assist Sue was Tom Wettengel, an ace American researcher who at first thought that Denis Compton was a quaint old Somerset village. Neither Sue nor Tom would have known a cricket story if it had jumped up and bitten them at long leg.

So I had the responsibility for drawing the cricket stories from Compo. He must have wondered what he had done to deserve to see so much of my ugly face, because every time he walked into his golf club, the *Express* office or local pub he found himself bumping into me. This went on for three years on and off before we finally got the show on the air. The first proposed programme was postponed because of the death of his brother, Leslie, and the second one following the passing of his old runmaking partner Bill Edrich.

Once the show was safely in the can ["One of the great nights of my life," was how Compo described it] got Denis and Keith Miller - as big a sporting god in Australia as Compton in England - reminiscing on some of their fascinating tales of the unexpected.

Sadly, Denis went to the great pavilion in the sky on St George's Day, 23 April 1997 before we could get into print. But the stories live on. And what stories! They tell the tale of a golden sporting age that will never be repeated, and they capture the personality [private as well as public] of the most charismatic sportsman ever to pull on a pair of cricket pads or football boots.

As I trawl through Compo's life and times on the following pages I have tried to keep a low profile, leaving it to an army of his old colleagues and friends to help paint the portrait of a sporting master of whom it can be fairly said that never has one man given so much pleasure to so many.

In return for the cooperation I have received in compiling the stories, I am making a donation to the Lord's Taverners, the charity organisation close to Compo's heart. My old Fleet Street colleague and chum John "Brommers" Bromley, later the innovative head of ITV Sport, is the current chairman of the Taverners. He was a long-time friend of Compo's and was the last to have an in-depth interview with him for a Bob Patience-produced documentary screened shortly after his death in April 1997 by London Weekend Television.

In my television sports column in the *Sun* I campaigned for the BBC to give Compo the farewell that he deserved. Brommers was the only man to come up with a fitting television tribute, and it was shameful that the BBC – with their rich archival material – did not do more to mark the passing of a sporting legend.

The collection of stories on the following pages reveals just why Compo was recognised as a national treasure. This is not a warts 'n' all portrait. It would be easy to dwell on his few failings, such as an at times too liberal liking for a glass or three, a fondness for gambling that occasionally bordered on the reckless, and a short temper that came with the pain that accompanied his old age. But I am not here to expose the scars on a hero. This is an unabashed celebration of Compo, his sporting life and times. I hope it reveals to the younger generations why the name Compton is held in such esteem by their fathers and grandfathers, whom I invite to wallow with me in bucketfuls of nostalgia for the days when

Compo filled the playing fields of England with his runs.

It took the Dean of Westminster, the Very Reverend Dr Wesley Carr, to orchestrate the most memorable and imaginative of all farewells to our hero. He was the driving force behind a stunningly splendid Service of Thanksgiving for the Life of Denis Compton, CBE, in the summer of 1997.

And this is where our story starts, with the sun out and Compo finishing his golden innings in front of a full house at Westminster Abbey.

1: Farewell Compo

*To watch Denis bat on a good day was
to know what joy was. He was a
wonderful ambassador for the game of
cricket and for our country.*
John Major

THE Thanksgiving Service for the Life of Denis Compton was over, and as we stepped out of Westminster Abbey into the sort of sunlight in which Compo used to quick-step to his centuries the fifty-somethings among us were filled with thoughts of short-trousered days when, with socks around our ankles and school ties askew, we would queue and jostle for The Great Entertainer's autograph. The sixty-somethings had clearer pictures on their memory screens, of his cavalier batting, his dribbling raids down the left wing and laughing approach to sport and to life. Those over seventy were his contemporaries who remembered him as a peer without equal.

All of us walked with just a little more spring in our step, saddened at his passing but buoyed by the fact that we had been lucky enough to share in his life, even if in most cases it was as spectators. We had run his runs with him, cracked his boundaries, beaten his full-backs, scored his goals, used his Brylcreem and suffered his agonies when his knee injury started the long, painful decline of his career.

Outside the Abbey there were many more than the two thousand who had been lucky enough to obtain tickets for the service. Scores of them had come to pay their respects even though they had been unable to get a ticket. There were stories of £50 offers being made for a pass into the Abbey. That would have greatly amused Compo. "Who wants two togevver?" would have taken him back to his halcyon days when the London ticket touts struck oil on the back of his

7

batting masterpieces. It was yet another 'house full' for Compo.

Tourists mingled with the people who had just given thanks for the life of the great all-rounder, and they were curious as to who it was who had managed to draw such a crowd, including a former prime minister, lords and ladies, knights, tycoons, sportsmen and stars of the stage and screen. More impressively, he had attracted a vast number of "ordinary" men and women whose lives he had enriched with his sporting prowess at a time when they were nearly on their knees after years of war and want. Compo had brought them to their feet, and now – fifty years on – they were paying their respects and saying their thanks. *Life's race well run, life's work well done. Now cometh rest.*

A Japanese tourist bowed politely after reading the Thanksgiving Service poster on the Abbey noticeboard. "Excuse please," he asked, "who is Denis Compton?"

"You do not have a long enough vacation for me to tell you," I wanted to reply. How do you begin to explain to a foreigner about Denis Compton? To an American you would say he was the Babe Ruth of cricket ... to a Brazilian you would say he could be mentioned in the same breath as Pele ... to an Argentine you would talk about him being Maradona without the drugs and certainly without the cheating .. to a Frenchman the Chevalier of cricket, full of *joie de vivre* ... to an Italian, the Pavarotti of the cricket field, with a complete aria of shots. And if an alien had arrived, you would have said he was our leader. To a Japanese? I just smiled and gave the admittedly biased, but totally accurate summary, "He was one of England's greatest ever sportsmen."

In the following pages I am, for the sake of accuracy, going to be generous to Compo's memory in the quotes from him. In truth, he was very hazy on moments that we recall as if they happened yesterday. "D'you remember, Denis, when you went down the wicket and lofted Doug Wright for successive sixes?" His face would light up, but not his memory. "Remind me, old boy," he would say, and as you recounted it the moment would fleetingly come to his mind and he would give an exact description.

While we were all busy counting his runs, Compo was much too busy scoring them to worry about and store little details like his 300 runs in 181 minutes being a world record that has lasted nearly fifty years, and the fact that eleven of his record eighteen centuries in 1947 came within the calendar months of July and August.

He confided that the main reason he called everybody "old boy" was that he had a terrible memory for names and did not want to offend them.

As the Westminster bells pealed joyously in Compo's memory, I looked back at the Abbey steps and took a panoramic view. To the left, Denis's widow, Christine, and their daughters Charlotte and Victoria, were looking charming in bright, beautiful clothes. No mourning here. They were remembering a husband and a father with unbounded delight. They looked a picture and did Denis proud. His sons from South Africa, Brian, Patrick and Richard, mixed with a Compton family having their first full reunion since the *This Is Your Life* night. Only Compo was missing, but you could sense that he was with them in spirit.

Former prime minister John Major was deep in conversation with Keith Miller, who was looking every one of his seventy-seven years. We were all lost in admiration for the obviously enormous effort he had made to get to the final farewell to Compo from his home in Australia. "Wild horses would not have stopped me being here to say goodbye to my old buddy," he said, with a sudden glint in his eyes that batsmen must have seen just before he bowled one of his lightning bouncers.

Among a dignified queue waiting to pay their respects to Christine and the family was a sea of famous faces including Lord (Colin) Cowdrey, Lord (Brian) Rix, Sir Tim Rice, Sir Alec

Bedser with twin brother Eric, Paul Getty II, Lords Archer, Griffiths, Howie, Kingsland, MacLaurin, Runcie and Vestey, actors Peter O'Toole and Albert Finney, author Leslie Thomas, entertainer Jimmy Tarbuck, and myriad current and former cricketers paying homage to a hero. I cannot think of any other sportsperson who could have attracted such a diverse cross-section of celebrities.

But even more telling was the way ordinary people who had never met Compo flocked to the Abbey to bid farewell to a man who had touched all their lives with his magical sporting skills.

It had been a moving (and at times amusing) memorial service, and the Abbey air was thick with Compo stories and tributes. Let us eavesdrop ...

The Laughing Cavalier

J.J. (JOHN) WARR, Compo's close friend for more than fifty years and a former president of the MCC and once captain of Middlesex, had the Abbey congregation rocking with laughter with a fittingly irreverent address: "If Compo had been alive during the Civil War he would definitely have fought for the Cavaliers. He certainly had a cavalier approach to two things: money and honours. For instance, the ribbon to his CBE medal was last seen acting as a temporary lead around the neck of Benjy, his Old English sheepdog. Compo had a natural talent for sport, but he was not the most industrious of people off the pitch. I remember that when Ted Heath's government introduced the three-day week during the miners' strike in 1974 I asked Compo how he was going to cope. He said, 'I am not going to work an extra day for anybody!' Batting with him was quite an experience. He was the only batsman who called for a single and wished you luck at the same time. He was a great improviser and totally untutored. If he ever read a coaching manual it must have been upside down. There has not been a more entertaining cricketer in the history of the game. Compo was delightfully disorganised, and his reputation for being in the wrong place at the wrong time came from using the back seat of his car as a filing cabinet. Invitations and letters were thrown there and forgotten. He once turned up at Heathrow as host for a tour party to Australia with an out-of-date passport and without a visa. The shepherd caught up with his flock in Melbourne four days later. His forgetfulness was just one of his many endearing qualities for which we all loved him."

Lasting friendship

KEITH MILLER, Compo's great rival on the pitch and best friend off it who had flown from Australia just to be at the service. "This was a wonderful gathering for a wonderful man. Compo watching from Up There will have been very pleased and proud ... that's if he got to the service on time to hear all the tributes! I was determined to get here for the service, even though my health's not been all that clever. It's called galloping old age. I spoke to Compo on the telephone from Australia the day before he died. His last words to me were, 'I'll see you in the Long Room and we'll have a couple of large drinks.' I've lost a soul mate. I doubt if two sportsmen on opposing sides have ever had a friendship that lasted as long as ours. We did our best to get the better of each other out on the cricket pitch, but once the final ball had been bowled we would adjourn to the nearest bar and have a drink and a laugh. There will never be another like Compo. We were closer than brothers."

Wonderful ambassador

JOHN MAJOR, former prime minister who declined an invitation to the handover of Hong Kong to make sure he was at the Abbey: "Denis would have been pleased to see so many smiles on the faces of the congregation as they remembered his dashing approach to cricket, football and to life. To watch him bat on a good day was to know what

11

joy was. He was a wonderful ambassador for cricket and for our country with his all-round ability and the sporting, friendly manner in which he always conducted himself. It is well known that I am a Surrey supporter, but Denis used to regularly claim my attention with his magnificent batting for both Middlesex and England. John Warr told an amusing true anecdote during his perfectly weighted address. We were in a reception room after a thanksgiving service for Brian Johnston here at Westminster Abbey when somebody asked Denis if he would like a drink. 'No, it's all right,' he said, 'the Prime Minister's getting me one.' I was very privileged to be getting a drink for Denis Compton, just as I am privileged to be here for this fond farewell to an outstanding British sporting idol. We will not see his like again."

Cricketing paradise

PETER O'TOOLE, one of Compo's many actor friends: "I have come here to Westminster Abbey to say farewell to a marvellous man and an outstanding sportsman. I was raised in the Yorkshire territory of the great Len Hutton, but always allowed myself a sneaking admiration for the cheerful and adventurous way Denis played the game. My old acting buddy Trevor Howard was a Compton freak, and they spent many hours together at the bar discussing the intricacies of cricket. Trevor used to have it written in his contracts that he must always have time off to watch the Test matches at Lord's and the Oval. No wonder, with Compton and Hutton together in the same team. They took us to a cricketing paradise."

Look but don't copy!

LORD (COLIN) COWDREY: "Denis was a particular hero of mine from when I first lifted a cricket bat. Coaches always used to stress, 'Enjoy watching him but don't try to play like him.' Nobody could imitate Denis. He had a style and an outlook all of his own. He had a wonderful mastery of batting but not a shred of arrogance. The fact that he could pack Westminster Abbey to capacity speaks volumes for the esteem in which he was held by his peers and the great British public."

Great ticket demand
DR WESLEY CARR, the Very Revered Dean of Westminster: "The demand for tickets to this Thanksgiving Service surpassed virtually anything that we can remember since broadcaster Richard Dimbleby's memorial service in 1966. We had to sadly turn down many hundreds of requests for tickets. The Compton family wanted this to be very much a service attended by the general British public with whom Denis had such a close rapport. The various ages of the congregation bears testimony to the impact of his life on several generations."

A shining light
LORD RUNCIE, of Cuddesdon, the former Archbishop of Canterbury: "I was privileged to play a role in this Thanksgiving Service for a man for whom I had great admiration both as a sportsman and as a person. For anybody from my generation Denis was a shining light in those bleak years immediately after the war. It was as if the sun shone every time Denis went to the wicket, and he cheered up the entire nation as we all used to enquire, 'How many runs did Denis get today?' The warmth we have all felt here in the Abbey today was generated by so many wonderful memories."

Carefree spirit
E.W. (JIM) SWANTON, the master of the microphone and a respected voice of cricket for more than fifty years: "I had the unforgettable experience of batting with Denis for Middlesex seconds against Kent at Folkestone in 1936. Even then as a youngster he had a carefree spirit and went for his

shots from the very first ball. As the senior batsman I took it upon myself to tell him to play up and down the line. He thanked me and then proceeded to sweep, cut and hook in that inimitable style of his. We shared a century stand, and on my return to Lord's I told Middlesex captain R.W.V. Robins that I had just been playing with the best young cricketer I had ever seen. Now here we are some sixty one years later at Westminster Abbey singing his praises and remembering the delight he brought to the cricket field. He lived up to everything I expected from him, and the extraordinary attendance here today shows that many, many people shared my view of him."

An adventurer
DENNIS SKINNER, Labour MP for Bolsover: "There is little doubt that Denis and I would have been poles apart politically, but this is not about politics. This is about saying farewell to a great Englishman, who performed wonders on the cricket field and was also a first-class footballer. I watched him play some wonderful stuff on those nippy Derbyshire pitches. He was a real adventurer, wasn't he? He took risks and went for runs right from the off. He was everything that Boycott wasn't."

The entertainer
SIR ALEC BEDSER: "What a marvellous service. Denis would have been thrilled to bits to see how much affection there is for him. We were good friends from back in the war years. I caught him out in the first match we played against each other, but I didn't have too much success against him in later years. When he was on top of his game he could take any bowling attack apart. He could never tell my twin brother Eric and I apart, and we used to have great fun pulling his leg. Denis was an entertainer on and off the pitch, and, speaking as one of his many victims, even being run out by him was a memorable experience."

14

A great crowd puller
SIR TIM RICE, songwriter, lyricist and cricket fanatic: "I am sure that Denis would have been late walking through the gates of Heaven, but a heartfelt 'Sorry, old boy' to St Peter would have earned instant forgiveness. Denis was as famous as any England cricketer has ever been, and he inspired affection in the least sentimental of men; but he was never, ever arrogant. The demand for tickets for this service was quite staggering. He remained a great crowd puller to the end."

Enormous impact
JIMMY TARBUCK, entertainer and all-round sports lover: "I was just a lad growing up in Liverpool when Denis was scoring all his centuries and dashing down the wing for Arsenal. In later years I got to know him, and what a smashing man! He was never boastful about all that he had achieved, and was more interested in talking about his golf. Just look at the turn-out here at the Abbey. It says everything about the man that so many people wanted to come and say, 'Cheerio Compo.' The remarkable thing is that he had not been active in sport for forty years. It just shows the enormous impact that he made, both with the cricket bat and the football."

Emptying the bars
FRED TITMUS, Compo's former Middlesex colleague: "Mike Atherton once asked me at an England team selection meeting, 'Just how good was Denis Compton?' I thought for a moment before saying, 'I can't tell you that, Mike, because you just wouldn't believe me.' I was not being deliberately evasive. I just didn't want Mike to think I was exaggerating. There are hundreds of people here at Westminster Abbey who will know what I say is true. Denis was a batting genius, pure and simple. Whenever he went in to bat the bars emptied and everybody in the dressing-

15

room would go out on to the balcony to watch because they knew they would see something extra special. In later years when he became President of Middlesex he would go out of his way to quietly find out the Christian names of visiting players, and then go and wish them luck with that nice personal touch that made them feel important. He was a class act as a cricketer and, more important, as a man."

Inspiring brothers
MIKE GATTING, former Middlesex and England captain: "Even though I did not see Denis play, the Compton name was revered in my household when I was growing up with my brother Steve. We were continually being told the stories of the Compton brothers and of their all-round achievements in cricket and football. They were a real inspiration to us. I joined Middlesex and Steve became a professional footballer. Denis was always coming into the Middlesex dressing-room to encourage us, and was very friendly and approachable. There cannot be many people who would attract such an enormous audience to their memorial service. It underlines just what a great hero he was ... and in two sports, too."

What a character
GODFREY EVANS, Compo's former England team-mate and close pal: "I can hear Compo having a good chuckle in the great dressing-room in the sky. We were all here on time, and I bet he arrived late for the service! He was a lovely, lovely man, and what a cricketer! There have been more stylish batsmen and more technically correct, but none to match him as an entertainer. He was nerveless and often had to be woken up from under the *Sporting Life* in the dressing-room to be told it was time to go out to bat. He would grab the first bat he put his hands on and go out and knock the bowling all over the field. When I went a world record ninety seven minutes without scoring in a match-

saving stand with him in Australia, he kept encouraging me by saying, 'Just play it straight, Godders. There'll be a nice couple of cold pints waiting for us once we've seen off these Aussies.' He managed to make it sound like the Promised Land. What a character. They definitely threw away the mould after making Denis."

Arsenal loyalist

PETER HILL-WOOD, Chairman of Arsenal Football Club: "It is an honour to be here representing Arsenal. Denis and his brother Leslie were great favourites at Highbury. But for the war, there is little doubt that Denis would have become an established international. He had to settle for wartime representative honours, while Leslie won two caps at the age of thirty-eight. They played together in our FA Cup-winning team against Liverpool at Wembley in 1950, and it is an indication of their loyalty that they spent their entire football careers with Arsenal and played County cricket only for Middlesex. Denis was, of course, best known as a cricketer, but there are many of his peers who consider that he would have been recognised as one of the finest of all outside-lefts but for the war."

Quite unique

LORD (JEFFREY) ARCHER, author: "Denis inspired an entire generation of schoolboys to pick up a cricket bat and try to become the next Denis Compton. Of course, there could only ever be one of him. He was quite unique. The proof that he touched the lives of many people he had never met is here in the Abbey today. It's a quite amazing gathering, so many famous faces yet also the man in the street with whom Denis had such a rapport through the magic of his batting."

A blazing light

TED DEXTER, former England cricket captain: "Along with thousands of other schoolboys, I idolised Denis. This was in the immediate postwar years when he brought sudden sunshine to a nation weary from war. He made it all look so easy, and played in a spirit that captured the imagination. I got to know him well, and he never disappointed me. It all seems like only yesterday when he was a blazing light in our game, and now here we are in Westminster Abbey paying a fond farewell to a great hero. What a wonderful send-off."

The Ashes regained

TOM GRAVENEY, Compo's former England team-mate: "It was 1953 when I played in the Test at the Oval in which Denis hit the winning run to regain the Ashes. Also here today from ~ team are Alec Bedser and Godfrey Evans, and dear old Keith Miller has managed to make it from Australia. The four of us will always have a very special bond with Compo, and it is extremely moving to be here in Westminster Abbey remembering one of the greats of our game. Our thoughts are with his widow, Christine, and his charming family. They must be enormously proud at the amazing size of the congregation and of the warmth of feeling for Denis that you can almost reach out and touch. By all accounts they could have filled the Abbey several times over for today's Thanksgiving Service. It is an indication of his standing not only in the world of sport but with the general public."

Overwhelmed

CHRISTINE COMPTON, Denis's widow: "We have been amazed and overwhelmed at the response to the service. We obviously knew that Denis had been a big favourite to a lot of people, but we did not realise that he was this big. Denis and I married some years after his sporting career had finished, and I was won over by his charm and personality. Now I know that many people had loved him dearly and had been won over in the same way. For myself and all Denis's family this was one of the most moving and memorable days of our lives, and we thank from the bottom of our hearts all those responsible for the organisation of the service. I know Denis would have been so pleased and proud."

Extremely moving

RICHARD COMPTON, Denis's youngest son from the second of his three marriages: "I have lived for most of my life in South Africa, and I obviously knew that Dad was a famous sportsman but I had no idea that he was this popular. After all, it is forty years since he participated as a professional cricketer. The demand for seats at the Abbey was just astonishing. I could not believe it, and find it extremely moving. It is a tribute to the British people as well as to Dad that they remember him so kindly. I don't wish to put any pressure on my son but there just might be another Compton coming through. Nicholas, who is fourteen, shows a definite aptitude for cricket and he is captain of his school team back home in Durban. We have told him many tales about his grand-father, and he is already day dreaming about possibly one day playing cricket here in England. There is nothing, I know, that would have pleased Dad more."

God bless, Compo

J.J. (JOHN) WARR gets the last word from the Abbey: "It was fitting that in the final weeks of Compo's life a comet appeared in the sky above Great Britain, for he was a comet in his own right, cascading brilliance wherever he went in the sporting firmament. Whenever he ended a telephone conversation, he would sign off, 'God bless' and I say, 'God bless you Compo for all the pleasure you gave to so many people.'"

As the congregation filed out of Westminster Abbey, the bells started to peal and you could almost hear them saying over and over again, "Thank you Compo ... Well played Compo."

We all basked in our personal memories of The Great Entertainer, and the days when he lit up the playing fields of England with his style and his smile. Leaving the Abbey, we all felt Compo's presence. I am sure I was not alone in playing an imaginary late cut, then the sweep before dancing down the wicket to hit the spinner for six. Compo may be gone but for many of us lucky to have seen him play and to have known him he will always be with us.

Ian Wooldridge, the Denis Compton of sportswriters with the *Daily Mail*, was my companion as we walked out into the sunshine. "Denis will be arriving just about now," he said, with a smile of affection for somebody who had been among the first to attract him to wanting to compose prose about sport. Compo was always a magnet for word artists who want to write about as well as watch the best.

I list the names of many of the people drawn to the service of remembrance in The Extras section, but now we go back to where it all started.

Come with me back to the days when young, short-trousered Compo started out with a lamppost as his wicket, the pavement as his pitch and dreams of playing at Lord's as his motivation.

2: The First Runs

*Nature came to Denis Compton with
her cornucopia pretty full, and she
let him help himself to it.*
Neville Cardus

DENIS CHARLES SCOTT COMPTON was born in Hendon, Middlesex, in the last year of the First World War on 23 May 1918. His father, Harry, was a self-employed house painter and decorator, and his mother, Jessie, a former housemaid who concentrated on bringing up their two sons, Leslie and Denis, and their daughter Hilda. They lived in a terraced house at 47 Alexandra Road in Hendon which was then considered Middlesex by the postman but now has a London NW4 postcode. To Denis, it was always Middlesex.

I was privileged to have Compo take me back in time to his formative years during our many conversations when he was unknowingly feeding me information for his *This Is Your Life* tribute from Eamonn Andrews. He recalled his boyhood days with almost misty-eyed nostalgia.

The road to glory

DENIS COMPTON: "Alexandra Road was my Wembley and my Lord's. In summer the lamppost close to my house was a wicket, and in the winter it provided the floodlight for our kick-around games in the road, with our jackets laid down as goalposts. It was safe in those days because you rarely saw a motor car. We were a poorish family, but I had an idyllic childhood. Dad encouraged both Leslie and me to concentrate on our sport. He had been a fair all-rounder, and was keen that we should play sport all year round because he said it was healthy for us. In my imagination I was Jack Hobbs when I was batting and Alex James when I was dribbling the ball. Mr Mitchell, the master in charge of my class at Bell Lane Elementary, told me when I was just twelve, 'Compton, judging by your schoolwork you are interested only in sport. Perhaps you should start thinking about earning your living at it.' There were chuckles round the classroom when I replied, 'I've already decided to do that, sir.' Instead of putting me down for being cheeky, Mr Mitchell took me under his wing and made me captain of both the school cricket and football teams. He and another master called, of all things, James Bond, were the first to see that I had been blessed with some sort of special gift. They were both very supportive when my exam marks clearly suffered because of the amount of time and effort I was putting into sport."

I first tapped into the life and times of Compo when employed as a sportsroom assistant at the London *Evening News* in 1955. E.M. (Lyn) Wellings, then the *News* cricket correspondent, assigned me to the job of reading through old newspaper files for background information for a supplement that he was secretly preparing after a tip-off that Compton's career was coming to an end because of his recurring knee problem. The following were among the stories I culled about the young Compo.

A natural talent
MARK MITCHELL, Compo's form master at Bell Lane Elementary School, which was situated within a six hit of Alexandra Road, gave this remarkably prophetic interview to the London *Evening Star* in 1931: "Young Compton has a natural talent on the sportsfield, whether it is with a cricket bat in his hand or a ball at his feet. Of all the hundreds of boys who have passed through this school, I have never known one so clearly destined to become a professional

sportsman. His reward of a Jack Hobbs bat from your newspaper could not have gone to a more deserving case. Frankly, his schoolwork suffers because he puts so much into sport. But this is one case when I think it is justified. I am sure he is going to be a great credit to our school and I will be surprised if he is not an established professional at both football and cricket before this decade is out."

The influence of Hobbs

HARRY COMPTON, Denis's father, talked about the Hobbs connection when interviewed in 1947 after Compo had beaten The Master's record of sixteen centuries in a season: "Winning a Jack Hobbs bat gave Denis the thrill of a lifetime. I had taken him to the Oval on several occasions to see the great man play for Surrey, and Denis made a point of studying him through my field glasses. I would say that Hobbs and his Surrey partner Andrew Sandham had the greatest influence on him, although Denis appeared to be developing a style all of his own. It was in Alexandra Road where he first showed his power with both the bat and the football. There is hardly a window down the road that I have not had to replace at one time or the other! 'Oh, that's Denis,' was the regular cry from neighbours. 'Call Harry in to mend the window.' Nobody really took offence because they could see that Denis was a budding talent even when he was still in short trousers. He played with me in the Bell Lane Old Boys' team that I captained when he was just twelve, and the opposing skipper said that his team did not take kindly to having to bowl to a tiny schoolboy because they were frightened of hurting him. I told him that his bowlers should play their natural game. They started off by bowling him dollies, but were soon going flat out trying to get rid of him. Denis scored forty-two runs off them!"

Leslie Compton will be a regular visitor to these pages, helping to paint the portrait of his younger brother. I met big

Les many times before his death at the age of seventy-two in Christmas week 1984. If anything, he was an even nicer person than Denis. He was the epitome of the gentle giant, four inches taller than Denis at six foot three and with a surprisingly high-pitched, Graham Gooch-like voice that carried the echo of a childhood spent in Essex. Denis had a deeper, more cultured voice that he deliberately cultivated for a broadcasting career after first adapting it to accept scores of invitations to "please say a few words". As mine host of a pub on Highgate Hill, Les was always willing to talk with warmth and not an ounce of envy about the extraordinary feats of his kid brother.

Blow football

LES COMPTON: "Denis and I were eaten up with sport when we were kids growing up in Hendon. I was six years older and much bigger, so when we played twopenny-halfpenny football on the kitchen table I insisted on being Arsenal, while he pretended to be West Ham. The Hammers were our second club because our parents had moved from Woodford in Essex where my sister Hilda and I were born. This was West Ham territory, and most of our family supported them. Denis was ambidextrous and used to get the better of me by playing two handed at twopenny-halfpenny football, so I decided we would play blow football instead. At last I'd found a game at which I could beat him. I always had more puff than Denis."

Brotherly love

DENIS COMPTON: "I could not have asked for a better brother than Les. Because he was that much older and wiser he was always protective of me. I've never forgiven myself for running him out in his testimonial match. I was particularly dithery that day and ran out no fewer than five of my Middlesex team-mates! When I ran out Leslie for a duck it was the closest he had ever come to hitting me. In fact he raised his bat like a sword, but it was all in fun. The crowd thought he was giving me a mouthful, but what he was saying was that I should make sure I stay at the crease for a long, long time to encourage people to come the next day, otherwise he would lose a packet at the gate. I dared not show myself in the dressing-room and followed Leslie's orders, and managed to get a hundred and plenty. I remember that I was in Australia when Les won his first England football cap at the age of thirty-eight in 1950. I called Nugget [Keith Miller] and we drank a bottle of champagne together in celebration. I was very proud of my brother. He became a top class bowls player after retiring from football and cricket, and was brilliant at any sport he turned his hand to. I owe a lot of my success to the support and encouragement that I got from Les. He was always there when I needed him."

The magic wand

LES COMPTON: "Denis was so busy running everybody out in my testimonial match that I thought it would all be over before we could get another day's play, but he occupied the crease long enough to ensure a big crowd for the final day. This was a time, remember, when a testimonial was all a player had as reward for loyalty. It was played against Sussex in the first week in June in 1954 and at one stage I thought it was going to be all over in two days thanks to Denis and his, what shall I say, eccentric running between the wickets. But he waved that magic wand of a bat of his, and we had a packed house on the third and final day to boost my testimonial to a handsome six thousand pounds. I knew from when he first started playing the game that I was not in the same class as a cricketer as Denis. He was a born genius."

It was a match for the London Elementary Schools XI against the Public Schools that changed Compo's life. The match was played on the Nursery pitch at Lord's on 13 September 1931 -often wrongly recorded as 1932. Denis was selected as opening bat and captain.

Bradman at his best

DENIS COMPTON: "I remember as if it were yesterday catching the number thirteen bus from Hendon and taking the threepenny half-price ride to Lord's, along with my proud schoolteacher Mr Mitchell. I was used to making the journey, but always to be a spectator or just to play in the nets. I even slept outside Lord's on a camp bed one night in 1930 to make sure I didn't miss seeing Don Bradman play for Australia against England in a Test match. He scored 254 in what he told me years later was his greatest innings. And I was there to see it, sitting on the grass at the Nursery End. What an experience. Now I was going to play at Lord's for real, rather than in my imagination. I opened the innings with a South London boy called Arthur McIntyre, who later became a magnificent wicketkeeper for Surrey. Arthur never let me forget that I ran him out!"

First of the run outs

ARTHUR McINTYRE, who had been born within a boundary hit of the Kennington Oval just four days before Compo's arrival in Hendon, served Surrey for more than forty years as player and then coach. He had vivid memories of the 1931 Lord's match: "Denis and I shared a century opening partnership before he ran me out. I was the first to hear his famous negotiation for a run. He pushed the ball to mid-on and then shouted 'Yes ... no ... sorry!' I had been backing up and was left stranded in no man's land. He was full of apologies in that naturally charming way of his in the dressing-room afterwards, and you just could not help but forgive him. It was all part of his appeal. Our cricketing paths crossed many times at both school and County level over the next twenty-five years. It was always a joy to be on the same pitch, even when it meant being behind the stumps watching him make huge totals. Cricket was fun when Denis was at the wicket."

A century at Lord's

DENIS COMPTON: "I managed to score 114 on what was the Nursery ground against the Public Schools, a real team of toffs who I recall were resplendent in multicoloured caps and pristine whites. I was wearing my first pair of long white flannels that my mother had bought specially for the game. I declared at two hundred and odd for eight, and then we whipped them out for just fifty-six. After our victory I was summoned to the pavilion to see Pelham Warner. 'Jolly good innings, Compton,' he said. 'Are your parents here?' The cat had got my tongue and I just nodded and blurted, 'Yes sir.' I hurried off and brought Mum and Dad to see him."

A mixed reception

PELHAM "PLUM" WARNER, knighted in 1937, was "Mr Cricket" at Lord's. He was a former England captain, led Middlesex before and after the First World War and later became a Test selector and President of the MCC. For him to summon Compo's parents was a call from the top of the mountain. He was later always proud to claim to have discovered Compo: "It was quite clear from the way that he batted against the public schools that this young lad had a natural gift for cricket, and I thought it would be of benefit to him to join the Lord's groundstaff. I was rather surprised to find that my idea got a mixed reception from his parents. Mr Compton was full of enthusiasm, but Mrs Compton was not at all sure. She was very concerned that he should have full-time employment, and seemed to think he would be better off trying for a career in the civil service on the clerical staff at Hendon Town Hall. Goodness me, what a crying shame that would have been for the world of cricket in general and for Middlesex and England in particular."

Sports-mad family

HILDA ADDINGTON, Denis's sister, gave me more background facts years later when attending Compo's *This Is Your Life* show: "Our mother was only doing what she thought was best for Denis. Funnily enough she got her wish with me because I went to work at the Town Hall and became the Mayor's secretary. Denis was a regular visitor there for celebration functions, and I don't think it's an exaggeration to call him Hendon's most famous and best-loved son. We were a sports-mad family, and I did quite well as a sprinter. But it was Denis who was the real star, and I'm glad to say that Mum and Dad lived to see his success. Mum passed on at 92, and Dad at 88. They were enormously proud of everything he did."

Mum's the word

MRS JESSIE COMPTON, Denis's mother, gave a different version of events in an interview during Compo's golden summer of 1947: "The story of how Denis joined the Lord's groundstaff has been misreported. Mr Warner, as he was then, did not ask us to make up our mind on the spot. He advised my husband to go home and think about it and we had a family conference. My concern was that I did not want Denis to have a job where he was employed for only four months of the year. My husband, of course, was keen as anything for Denis to play for Middlesex. It was Leslie who came up with the solution. He was then a young professional at Highbury and said that he would have a word with the famous manager Herbert Chapman about giving Denis a football trial."

Best of both worlds

DENIS COMPTON: "I am a bit vague about exactly what happened, but I believe that both Sir Pelham and Leslie told the legendary Herbert Chapman about the dilemma. Arsenal scouts had already seen me playing in England schoolboy trials and for Hendon and Middlesex schools, and Mr Chapman said that he would be happy to have me join the Highbury groundstaff when I was not needed at Lord's. I had been given the best of both worlds and even Mum could not put up an argument to that."

The Chapman connection
LES COMPTON: "To be honest, I would not have dared approach Mr Chapman. I was in Arsenal's reserves, and even established first-team players would have thought twice about talking directly to the man who was Mr Arsenal. You waited until he spoke to you first. I told our trainer Tom Whittaker about Denis, and it was he who passed it on to Mr Chapman. I think Arsenal had already made up their minds to take Denis on because he had been impressing our scouts for several seasons and had shown up well in senior games with Hampstead, which later became the famous Hendon amateur football club."

So Denis left school at fourteen for the dream double of going to Lord's in the summer and Highbury in the winter. He had been an average pupil at Bell Lane Elementary, but an honours student if measured in sporting terms.

Groundstaff boy
DENIS COMPTON: "My starting pay at Lord's in that summer of 1932 was twenty-five shillings a week, and, boy, did they get their money's worth. I had to report every morning at eight o'clock, and the first duty was to join the other groundstaff boys in hauling the heavy roller. It was a job for carthorses. If there had been a game the day before we would have to sweep the terraces, and then clean the boots of the players, tidy the dressing-rooms, mix the whitewash to paint the popping-creases and work the scoreboards. We used to supplement our wages by selling twopenny scorecards for a halfpenny commission, and, best of all, could pick up cash

tips for bowling in the nets to Lord's members. I remember once bowling to an aristocratic-looking gentleman, whose face was familiar. He balanced two half-crown coins on the top of the stumps in place of bails, and said that I could have them if I could knock them off. I managed to dislodge them with about my tenth ball, and I was five bob richer. It turned out that the gentleman was C. Aubrey Smith, who had been a first-class cricketer with Sussex before starting a distinguished acting career in Hollywood. That was the fun side of things in the nets, but our coaching sessions were deadly serious. I got the best coaching that any young cricketer could wish for."

The Natural

GEORGE FENNER was the first coach to work with Compo at Lord's. This was his 1947 assessment: "I am pleased to say that I managed to leave Denis pretty much as I found him. He had so much natural ability that I considered he was best left alone. It is always said that he is unorthodox, but if you study him closely you will see that there is a very sound technique at the foundation of everything that he does. Even when he hits across the line of the ball with that trademark sweep shot of his he is fully aware of his position and his balance is just perfect. I first realised that he was something very special when he used to play for my Nippers team, a side selected from the groundstaff for friendly Sunday matches. I knew that he would not be around in my team for long. There was a maturity about his batting that made him stand out, and even though many of his shots were of the invented variety everything came together to make an outstanding overall impression. He was quickly promoted to the Middlesex seconds, and within eighteen months he was in the first team. It was obvious that he had the potential to play at the highest level, and I considered even when he was just seventeen or so that it was just a question of time before he was a Test player."

A diamond unearthed

ARCHIE FOWLER was the head coach at Lord's, who took over from George Fenner as Compo's mentor: "I inherited this spirited young lad whose batting technique was all his own work, yet extremely effective. I decided very quickly that I should not interfere too much with his style, but to mix in as many fundamentals of straight-bat technique as I dare. He was a quick and enthusiastic learner, and within a season of working with him I was telling everybody that this was a diamond of a prospect. Denis more than lived up to all my expectations."

Testing time in the nets

DENIS COMPTON: "I cannot speak too highly of Archie Fowler. George Fenner gave me a foundation, but it was Archie who built on it and taught me so many things that served me well throughout my career. He helped me not only with my batting but my bowling. Archie had the gift of being able to get through to you without blinding you with science. I was later introduced to the joys of leg-spin bowling by Jack Walsh, Leicestershire's Australian spinner. He said I would get much more fun out of leg spin than orthodox. That's all the encouragement I needed to switch to leg spin. For me, fun was an important part of the game. I guessed that I must have been making good progress with the bat because Archie kept bringing top-flight players like Gubby Allen, Percy Fender, Arthur Wellard, Patsy Hendren and Walter Robins to test me out and encourage me in the nets. You could not buy that sort of experience, and it did wonders for my confidence."

A hero's bat

PATSY HENDREN had been the leading middle-order batsman in English cricket during the 1920s and was a hero to Compo, who was particularly impressed at the way he was able to combine a career in cricket and football. Patsy, a larger than life character with a roguish cockney sense of humour, was nearly as big an influence on Denis as coach Archie Fowler: "From the first time I clapped eyes on Denis with a bat in his hand I knew the boy was going to be one of the game's greats. The fact that it was one of the bats that carried my name helped me warm to him! I autographed it for him, and he continued to play with it for quite a few seasons. I was coming to the end of my career when he was just starting out on his, and what I liked about him was his willingness to listen to the old pros and learn from our experiences. It was not only his free-flowing strokes that made him stand out as a youngster, but also his attitude. He was bubbling with enthusiasm, and was always wanting to know how he could improve. Denis was also in love with the whole atmosphere of the game, and was always urging me to tell him stories about the good old days when I was a regular in the England team with the likes of his heroes Hobbs and Sutcliffe. I agreed with coach Archie Fowler's approach to Denis, and that was that here was a natural player who did not need coaching as much as just a few tweaks here and there to make sure his technique was right. A coach who tried to stick by the book with Denis just might have ruined one of the greatest prospects I had ever seen."

Mixed in with the spectacular strokes, run outs, eccentric shots and rapid scoring that go to make up the cocktail of the Compton legend is the little matter of forgetfulness. He showed this occasionally confusing, often frustrating and usually amusing trait when called up for his first representative game for the MCC against Suffolk at Felixstowe in the summer of 1934. It was an unforgettable start to his career.

A first-ball duck

DENIS COMPTON: "As the train pulled into Felixstowe station all the players reached up for their bags and bats on the racks above them. Suddenly I had a sickening feeling as I realised that I had left the bag that Mum had packed so carefully for me behind at Lord's. I had arrived without bat, boots, pads and whites. I was close to tears, but the old Hampshire professional George Brown said that I should not worry because I could borrow his gear if mine had not arrived from Lord's in time. George just happened to be six inches taller than me and twice as wide. As luck would have it, wickets fell rapidly and I found myself going into bat wearing boots that were three sizes too big, pads that came up under my armpits and rolled-up trousers and a flapping shirt that had room for another person. Not surprisingly, I failed to get George Brown's tree trunk of a bat to the first ball and my middle stump was knocked flat. I wanted the earth to open up and swallow me as I made the long journey back to the dressing-room, slipping and sliding in dear old George's big boots."

Denis was reunited with his own bat for the second innings and proceeded to accumulate 110 runs in dashing style. He dipped into his pocket for his handkerchief during the innings and fished out a note from Lord's groundsman Harry White that read, "One of these days young man you will forget your head! Good luck." The Compton legend was up and running.

3: Out for a Penny

Denis should not have had a normal birth. He should have been borne down from Valhalla on a silver cloud.
J.J (John) Warr

IT was for his bowling rather than his batting that Denis was selected by Middlesex for his County debut against Sussex at Lord's during Whitsun weekend 1936, a week after his eighteenth birthday. Skipper Walter Robins tossed him the ball as first-change bowler, and he trapped Harry Parks with his orthodox slow left arm bowling for his first of 647 first-class victims. Batting at number eleven, he came through the Players' gate (there was a separate entrance for the amateurs) and joined former England captain Gubby Allen with twenty runs needed for a first-innings lead.

On sacred ground
DENIS COMPTON: "You need to have cricket in your blood to understand how I felt making that first lonely walk out on to what I considered sacred ground. For non-cricketing people I can only describe it as the equivalent of making a solo entrance on to a great stage such as the Palladium or Covent Garden. My heart was thumping like a bass drum as I closed the Players' gate behind me. I had no problems about there being separate entrances for professionals and amateurs. It was just the norm. We even had separate dressing-rooms. G.O. Allen, one of the great amateurs who had often bowled to me in the nets, came from his crease to meet me. Waiting to bowl to me was an England legend in Maurice Tate."

A word of advice

G.O. (GUBBY) ALLEN, one of the leading fast bowlers of the inter-war era, followed Pelham Warner as a god-like figure at Lord's. He captained England and later became Chairman of Selectors and Treasurer and President of the MCC. Gubby, Australian born and Eton educated, was to become one of Compo's close friends, and had already tipped him as a future Test player when Denis first joined him at the wicket in his County debut: "I knew Denis quite well by then from the nets and realised that he would be nervous, yet quite capable of facing up to the Sussex attack. To be quite frank, I did not fancy our chances of getting a first-innings lead. I was playing with a dislocated finger, and this made it even more of an ordeal for Denis in his debut. I wished him luck, and gave him just one line of advice. 'Make sure you play forward to Maurice Tate.'"

The famous feet

DENIS COMPTON: "I had grown up with stories of the bowling performances of Maurice, and of how the ground used to tremble under his enormous boots. In the cuttings book that my parents used to keep there were several cartoons by Tom Webster of his boots looking like barges. I found my eyes drawn to his feet as I walked past him towards the wicket. 'Good luck, lad,' he was kind enough to say, 'but remember that it's my job to try to get you out.'"

Distinguished career

MAURICE TATE, one of the first medium-fast bowlers fully to exploit the use of the seam, was just coming to the close of his distinguished career. This was how he recalled the first balls bowled to Compo in County cricket: "Denis had already received quite a lot of publicity in the London evening papers and so we knew that he was something of a prodigy. I don't know if Denis felt nervous, but if he did he showed no signs of it. As I remember it, I wished him luck because he was just starting out on his career while mine was winding down. The game needed new blood, and from all that we had heard he was an outstanding prospect. I held nothing back and managed to beat him with my first two balls. Down at my end Gubby Allen shouted, 'Play forward, lad. Forward!'"

The first touch

DENIS COMPTON: "I did not get a sniff of the first two balls that Maurice bowled as he forced me on to the back foot. My anxious partner, Gubby Allen, was miming the forward defensive shot. The third ball swung in the air like a boomerang. It was a real Maurice Tate special. I moved forward MCC-coaching style and met the ball with the middle of the bat, killing it dead. That first touch was one of the most satisfying moments I had ever experienced. It gave me a whoosh of confidence, and I turned the next ball to third man for a comfortable single. We started to gather runs in ones and twos, and I was confident enough to steer Jim Parks to square leg for my first boundary in County cricket. Jim, brother of my first bowling victim Harry and father of wicketkeeper Jim, applauded the shot. That's the sort of sportsmanship that was commonplace in those days. There was a huge roar from the crowd when we passed the Sussex total to gain a first-innings lead."

After Compo had contributed fourteen runs to a last-wicket stand of thirty-six, Jim Parks got one to straighten and the ball rapped against his left pad. There was what was little more than a half-hearted appeal, and – as much to the surprise to the bowler as the batsman – umpire Bill Reeves lifted his finger.

The call of nature

GUBBY ALLEN: "As we walked off, I said to the umpire, a great character, 'You have just cheated that boy out of his wicket.' He looked at me sheepishly and admitted, 'I know the lad was not out, sir. But you've got your first innings lead ... and I'm dying to spend a penny.'"

Blades of humour

DENIS COMPTON: "Actually, I think Bill used a stronger phrase than that. He could use some ripe old language, and was famous for his wit. A favourite story in the Middlesex dressing-room was of the day R.W.V. [Walter Robins] removed his County sweater with its famous three scimitars and handed it to Bill, who tied it around his waist. Robbie, who was an extremely competitive individual, was in a foul mood at the end of a loose over and stalked away from the wicket. 'What about your sweater, Mr. Robins?' called Bill. 'You know what you can do with it,' snapped Robbie. 'What,' said Bill, 'swords and all, sir?'"

Young Compo was rewarded for his fourteen-run debut performance in a rain-ruined match with selection for the next County game against Nottinghamshire. This brought him face to face with famed and feared fast-bowling partners Harold Larwood and Bill Voce, who had been in the eye of the Bodyline storm in Australia three years earlier. It is part of Compo folklore that Denis, going in at number eight, hooked a Larwood bouncer to the boundary.

Hooking Larwood

DENIS COMPTON: "You could almost see the steam coming out of Harold as I stood up to him and drove him for two successive fours. My skipper Walter Robins was batting with me, and he came down the wicket and warned, "Now be careful ... there's a bouncer coming your way." Sure enough, Harold unleashed a bouncer and I timed a hook shot perfectly and cracked the ball to the boundary. I had never faced such fast bowling in my life, and decided I was best off attacking rather than going into a defensive shell. That was never my style. I was lucky at Middlesex to play with the great Patsy Hendren, who was coming to the end of his career. He was one of the finest players of the hook shot there has ever been. I learned by watching him and listening to his advice that you should not duck a rising ball but stand up to it and hook. Harold Larwood, God bless him, gave me a nod of acknowledgement each time I connected. I can honestly say that I could hear the ball whistling past my ears. That's how fast it was going. I was unbeaten on twenty-six at the end of the innings, but when I was promoted to number three in the second innings Harold got me leg before with a rip snorter when I had scored fourteen. I was always ready to argue that there has never been anybody faster."

While writing for the *Daily Express* in the 1960s through to the 1970s, I established a column called *Sports Forum* in which I put readers' questions to sports personalities. One question was: "Did Denis Compton ever play against Harold Larwood?" This gave me the excuse to contact Harold in Australia, to where he had emigrated in 1949. Despite more than twenty years living among the old "enemy", Harold's accent was still pure Nottinghamshire.

A reet good 'un
HAROLD LARWOOD: "I clearly recall playing against Denis in what was either his second or third County game for Middlesex. You don't quickly forget a youngster hitting three of your balls to the boundary after only just coming to the wicket. I said to Bill Voce as we came off at the end of that first innings, 'This lad's a reet good 'un.' I watched his career closely from then on, and I was not surprised to see him rival Wally Hammond, Jack Hobbs and Len Hutton as the greatest of all English batsmen. What I liked about Denis was he was always looking to play his strokes. This not only made him good to watch but also gave bowlers hope that he might slip up. Another thing I liked about him was that

he never got conceited and arrogant like some of those snooty amateurs who used to look down their noses at you. He was a player like us and treated us with respect. I was a lad from the mines and hated all that 'them and us' nonsense and being treated like second-class citizens. There were some amateurs who wouldn't even have you eating at the same table as them. We used to have a saying in the Notts dressing-room, "Let's go and knock their hyphens out." But Denis always had time for you, and I look forward to his visits to Australia where he is enormously popular. They always say out here that he is a Pom who played the game with an Australian spirit."

Denis experienced the highs and lows of cricket in his next match against Northampton, going for a first-ball duck in the first innings and then sharing a 129-run fifth wicket stand with skipper Walter Robins in the second. He contributed eighty-seven runs on his way to becoming the youngest player ever to score a thousand runs in a season. He was not only learning about batting but also about strict discipline in an era when the amateurs were known as "gentlemen" and the professionals as "players".

Humiliating experience
DENIS COMPTON: "I was never bothered by that gentlemen and players business. I just accepted it as part of cricket's rich tradition, and was happy always to address my seniors as 'sir' or 'Mister'. Even at Arsenal I called the likes of Alex James Mr. James, even though we were playing in the same team. They were days when you dare not answer back, and you showed respect to your elders. Mind you, the discipline could be tough to take at times. I remember playing in front of a packed crowd at Lord's in one of my early County matches when I dropped a skier while fielding in the deep. Our skipper R.W.V. Robins beckoned to me. 'Compton, get off the field immediately and come back on wearing a cap,'

39

he snapped. 'You will always wear a cap when the sun is shining and you are playing for me. Now off you go at the double.' He always demanded that you move at the double, particularly between overs. I felt myself going the colour of the cricket ball as I dashed back to the dressing-room for my cap. It was quite a humiliating experience, but I understood that the skipper was teaching me a lesson. I might have taken the catch had I been wearing a cap."

Exceptional prospect
R.W.V. (WALTER) ROBINS, former Middlesex captain and England Test selector, later became one of Compo's close friends. His strict discipline was all designed to help shape Denis into a master cricketer: "It was quite clear from his earliest games with Middlesex that Denis was an exceptional prospect, but we decided to protect him by playing him down the order. He needed experience, but without the pressure of having to make big scores. We were delighted with his progress, and it was obviously only a matter of time before he scored his first century. The manner in which it came was, to say the least, quite surprising."

Last-wicket stand
DENIS COMPTON: "I went in at number eight at Northampton, with all our established batsmen back in the pavilion and not too many runs on the board. Jim Sims and I put on seventy-six for the ninth wicket, and then last man Ian Peebles came in to join me. Ian was a fine bowler, but even he would admit that he was not exactly the world's greatest batsman."

Weight of responsibility
IAN PEEBLES, Aberdeen-born leg break bowler, writer and *bon viveur*, had his cricket career finished by a Second World War air raid that cost him the sight of an eye. He always looked back on his last-wicket stand with Compo as one of

the highlights not just of his career but of his life: "I was what you might generously call a specialist number eleven. It was evident that Denis was in unbeatable form, and I felt a great weight of responsibility. I was determined to try to hang around as long as possible. Even in those early days Denis had a presence at the wicket that inspired you to, if not meet his standards, then at least try to keep your wicket intact while he harvested the runs. I was cast in the role of labourer to the master craftsman. It was really nerve racking as he sailed towards his first century. One mistake by me, and he would miss out. I had never played with a straighter bat, nor with greater concentration. I sensed history in the making: Denis Compton's first century. We all knew that it would be the first of many. I was Sherpa Tenzing to Edmund Hillary. I was there when he climbed his Everest for the first time."

First County century

DENIS COMPTON: "Ian played a magnificent supporting role, giving me every opportunity to collect runs. I completed my century with my fifteenth boundary, and went down the wicket to say a special thanks to Ian who contributed eleven runs to our partnership of seventy-four. It was the start of what was to become a lifelong friendship during which I was able to enjoy Ian's wit and wisdom. He described it as the greatest innings he had ever played. I would not have completed my first century that day without him, and dear old Jim Sims."

Standing ovation

JIM SIMS, best known as a leg-break bowler but an attacking lower-order batsman, helped Compo lay the foundation to this first century: "I was as pleased as punch for Denis. That first century is such an important milestone for all cricketers. I had put on seventy-six with him for the ninth wicket, most of the runs coming from Compo's bat. When I was out, he still needed sixty runs for his hundred. No disrespect to last man in Ian Peebles, but you would have bet all the money in the world that there was no way that Denis was going to reach three figures. After all, even Ian considered himself a non-batsman. It was amazing how Denis managed to keep farming the bowling, protecting Ian and hitting every loose ball to the boundary. It was an incredibly mature performance for somebody so young and inexperienced. He got a standing ovation when his fifteenth boundary gave him his century. It was remarkable when you think that he went in at number eight. Few players in history could have scored a maiden century when going in so far down the order. Denis was always in control of his shots, and could get the ball to the boundary by following it with his eye almost past the stumps before just dabbing it. That, to me, was real artistry."

The first Compton century did not bring a victory. A thunderstorm washed out play with Northants eight wickets down and teetering on the brink of defeat. Northants skipper Vallence Jupp later presented Denis with the ball, specially mounted and engraved to mark his first century. He was now established as a County batsman. Already, he was being talked about as a Test prospect.

4: Taking the Test

*Denis Compton lit up so many summers for me
that I used to call him Mr. Sunshine.*
Trevor Howard

THE first of seventy-eight Test calls for Denis came in the summer of 1937. He was selected for the third and final Test against New Zealand starting at the Oval on 14 August 1937. At 19 years and 84 days, he was England's youngest ever Test cricketer. His official letter from the MCC Secretary confirming his selection arrived at his Hendon home the morning after he had heard the news on the wireless. It was typical of the formalities of the time that the letter started, "Dear Compton ..."

A dream come true
DENIS COMPTON: "We used to have a saying in the Army, 'I don't care what you call me as long as it's in time for breakfast.' That's how I felt about that letter. I did not care that it was stiff and formal. As far as I was concerned it was the greatest letter I had ever received. A few weeks earlier I had bought my first ever car, a little second-hand Austin Seven that cost me thirty-five pounds. I drove myself from North to South London, with my dad sitting alongside me almost too swollen with pride to fit into the car! It was not only my dream that had come true, but Dad's too."

Looking the part
HARRY COMPTON: "We concentrated on making sure that Denis had everything with him. As always for a big game, I

43

re-studded and whitened his boots and oiled his bats, while my wife took extra care over his flannels and shirt. I have always drummed into Denis that the cricketer who tries to look the part will play the part. I was a keen club cricketer for years, and Denis, Leslie and I would spend hours talking about batting and bowling tactics. Denis might give the impression that he is playing everything off the cuff, but he quietly gives a lot of thought to both his batting and bowling. Even with all that he had on his mind, he was thoughtful enough that when we arrived at the Oval he made sure I had found my way to my seat before he went off to the dressing-room to meet his new England team-mates."

Strongly recommended
DENIS COMPTON: "My skipper at Middlesex, Walter Robins, was also captain of the England team and, I know, had strongly recommended that I should be selected. Walter introduced me to my new England team-mates, including players I had queued to watch just a few years earlier such as Walter Hammond, Charlie Barnett and Les Ames. Cyril Washbrook and Austin Matthews were also making their debuts, and a young Yorkshireman called Len Hutton was a veteran of two Tests."

Ready for the challenge
WALTER ROBINS: "I had been pressing for Denis to be included in the Test team for some time, but the view was that we should not rush him too quickly at a time when young Leonard Hutton was being bedded into the team. We knew that players such as Hutton, Compton, Edrich and Washbrook were the future of the England team. We had to accept that the golden years of Hobbs, Sutcliffe and Hendren were behind us. Now was the time to start blooding our outstanding crop of young prospects. I was convinced that Denis was ready for the challenge of Test cricket. Having studied him closely since he first walked through the gates

at Lord's I knew better than anybody that he not only had the talent but the temperament to succeed at the top. The young Compton did not seem to have any nerves at all, but those of us close to him knew that he worried about his game much more than he ever let on. He gave a great deal of thought to each innnings, even though it looked as if he just went out and improvised. In the dressing-room he would always ask any incoming batsman what the wicket was doing and how so-and-so was pitching the ball. Denis was nowhere near as casual about his cricket as he appeared. We had seen to it from his earliest days at Middlesex that he grew up with all the right attitudes and disciplines. I knew that he was properly prepared to play at the highest level, and I had no hesitation in putting his name forward for Test duty."

New Zealand won the toss on the first morning of the scheduled three-day match, and Denis spent his first day in Test cricket in the field wearing his new size seven-and-one-eighth England cap. He never needed a larger size throughout his seventy-eight-Test career. In these early days before injury handicaps and increased weight he was a gazelle in the field with an eye for knocking down the stumps with long-range left-arm throws perfected by hours of practice.

Working too hard
ARCHIE FOWLER: "Everybody always referred to the young Denis as a natural, tending to forget that when first making his breakthrough he was one of the most energetic and conscientious trainers in the game. He was one of the few cricketers that I occasionally had to tell to stay away from the nets because he was working too hard. Then he would go away to a corner of the field and work on his own at fielding, and he developed a fine throwing arm. He could throw with either hand, but it was his left that he always favoured. His enthusiasm used to shine out of him like a searchlight. Yes, he is a natural but every youngster should

learn from him that it is the effort you put in off the pitch that counts as much as what happens out in the middle."

Time and again in researching this book I found it chronicled that Compo had carelessly run himself out in his Test debut. It is true that the scorebook reads, "Compton run out 6", but his dismissal owed nothing to his infamous suicidal tendency between the wickets.

Now let justice be done ...

A freak run out

DENIS COMPTON: "That run out in my Test debut was a pure freak. I went in with England in a spot of trouble at thirty-odd for two. It became more serious when just a few runs later Cyril Washbrook joined Len Hutton and Charlie Barnett back in the pavilion with only thirty-six on the board. I was then joined by the classical Notts strokemaker, Joe Hardstaff, and we had put on 125 for the fourth wicket when Joe stepped forward and cracked a straight drive off the bowling of Giff Vivian for what seemed a certain four. I was backing up and looked back in horror to see the ball crack against Vivian's outstretched hand and deflect on to the wicket. Because of my record in the running out department, I liked to tell people that I had been deflected out rather than run out."

Soft-hands technique

JOE HARDSTAFF was regarded as the most elegant batsman of his generation. He was remarkably consistent, scoring over 1,000 runs in a season thirteen times for Nottinghamshire and topping 2,000 four times. I talked to him about the Compo run out incident and, more than thirty years on, he absolved Denis of all blame: "I was devastated when Denis was run out through no fault of his own. He had been looking set for a century in his debut, and it was a cruel way to get out when he was so on top of the New Zealand bowlers. As

46

he walked off he raised his bat to me and wished me luck. I went on to make a hundred, and he was one of the first to congratulate me when I returned to the dressing-room. People often compared the way Denis and I batted, but while some of our strokes may have looked similar we had vastly different grips and our bats were very much to our own taste. Denis thought mine weighed a ton. It was a two pound seven ounce bat compared to the lightweight two pound three ouncer wielded by Denis. I liked to feel I had a heavy weapon in my hands, so that I could get real power into my shots. Denis had a soft-hands technique, and was more of a guider than a thrasher of the ball."

A few weeks later Hardstaff and Compton were on opposing sides at Trent Bridge, where Joe was following his legendary father, Joe Snr, as the king of Notts. Middlesex needed to win to snatch the County Championship from Yorkshire. Victory seemed certain when Notts were forced to follow on after Middlesex had built a 539-run mountain before declaring for the loss of nine wickets. Notts started their second innings 223 runs behind, and back home at Lord's champagne was being put on ice for celebrations of an anticipated championship triumph and the end of Yorkshire's monopoly of the title.

The long handle
DENIS COMPTON: "As Joe came out to bat the second time around our wicketkeeper Fred Price made the grave mistake of greeting him with the words, 'What d'you think of the new champions, Joe?' Oh dear. That was like a red rag to Joe. I was one of the bowlers he carted all around Trent Bridge on his way to an unbeaten double century. He singlehandedly forced a draw and stopped us taking the championship. Yorkshire owed him their title. I often recall that innings when I meet his son, Joe, who has become Secretary of Middlesex. His father was a corker of a batsman,

who had the highest grip of any batsman I ever saw. His gloves were right at the top of the handle and you would have thought a fast ball would have knocked the bat out of his hands. But as he kept blasting me to the boundary I realised just what was meant by 'giving it the long handle'."

Denis returned to Highbury in the winter of 1937–8 to continue laying the foundations to his football career after making his First Division debut for Arsenal at the age of eighteen. He was back at Lord's in the summer of 1938, ready and eager to establish himself in the England Test team against Don Bradman's Australian tourists. Following a 3–2 Ashes defeat in Australia, the selectors had decided to start building their team round the young talent of exceptional prospects like Len Hutton, Bill Edrich, Doug Wright and, of course, Denis Compton. Bill and Denis, inseparable even then, made the trip to Nottingham together by train and found themselves housed on the eve of the first Test in the same hotel as the Australians.

Bedtime gamesmanship
DENIS COMPTON: "The Aussies could not have been friendlier, and Don Bradman led a squad of them who came up to me in the hotel to wish me good luck. I had a fascinating two-hour session in the room shared by Bill 'Tiger' O'Reilly and Chuck Fleetwood-Smith, two of their exceptional bowlers. They entertained me with stories of cricket Down Under, but then as I prepared to go to bed Bill could not resist a bit of gamesmanship. 'Just sleep on this, young Denis,' he said. 'Smithy and I have cooked up something very special for you tomorrow. We want you to have a great career, mate, but not at our expense. Sorry, but we're going to see to it that you go cheaply.' He said it with a grin on his face, but I knew that he meant every word. I've never met an Aussie yet who would let a Pom take runs off him without one hell of a fight."

It was the second day before Denis walked to the Trent Bridge wicket for his debut against Australia. Len Hutton had occupied the middle for much of the first day on the way to his first century against the old enemy. He, too, was making his debut against Australia. Hutton and Gloucestershire opening master Charlie Barnett put on a then record 219 for the first wicket. Hutton, Bill Edrich, Barnett and skipper Wally Hammond all lost their wickets in quick succession, and England had suffered a minor slump to 281 for four when Denis joined Lancashire's Eddie Paynter at the wicket.

Waiting to bowl to him was Tiger O'Reilly.

Dropped by Bradman

DENIS COMPTON: "As I walked past him, Tiger gave me that roguish grin of his and said, 'Good luck, Denis, but remember what I said. You're going cheaply.' He surrounded me with fielders, and I edged his third ball to none other than Don Bradman, who put down what was a difficult chance. O'Reilly was without question one of the greatest bowlers I ever faced. You never knew what to expect from him. He could make the ball spin viciously, go straight on, loop in the air or bounce like a tennis ball. People used to say I was relaxed at the wicket, but never against Big Bill. He tried to take your wicket with every ball, and you were dead if you did not concentrate."

The young rascal

BILL "TIGER" O'REILLY was one of the great characters of cricket, who later became a respected writer on the game: "I tried every trick I knew to get Denis out in his debut against us. The Don put down a tough chance, and from then on Denis did not give us a look in. He played a magnificent innings, and I hated him for it! Denis and Eddie Paynter really put us through the wringer just as we thought we were getting on top. Denis and I became good mates off the field, but we made him battle for every one of his runs. He knocked me about a bit at Trent Bridge, but I'd like it put on record that I did manage to get the young rascal's wicket five times that summer."

Compo scorched to his maiden Test century against the Australians, sharing what was a record fifth-wicket partnership of 206 in just 138 minutes with Eddie Paynter. During the tea interval on his way to his hundred, skipper Wally Hammond told him, "If you get your hundred, take a fresh guard and then put your mind to getting a second hundred." When he had reached 102 and acknowledged a standing ovation from the Trent Bridge crowd, Denis tried to sweep leftarmer Fleetwood-Smith for his sixteenth boundary and was brilliantly caught in the deep. There was one face as black as thunder among the team-mates applauding him back into the dressing-room.

A rollicking from Hammond

DENIS COMPTON: "Wally Hammond was absolutely livid. 'Never, never,' he said, 'give your wicket away to an Australian. I told you to take a fresh guard. Well done, but in future do what you're told.' To be honest, I never ever got on to the same wavelength as Hammond. He was a man of dark moods, and you could never get close to him. However, he had my full respect as an outstanding batsman, and I accepted that he meant well with the rollicking that he gave me at what was one of the proudest moments of my life. When I think of Wally I always have a laugh to myself about something that Eddie Paynter once said about him. Eddie was an outspoken and at times very comical Lancastrian. A journalist asked him for his assessment of Hammond. Eddie thought for a while, looking off in the distance as if recalling one of Wally's magnificent knocks. Then he replied, 'Ah, Wally, yes ... now there was a man who liked a good shag.' It's true that he desired the company of pretty women and could drink most of his team-mates under the table, but my first assessment of him would be that he was a master batsman who did not know how to handle people. I had enormous admiration for him as a cricketer, but he did not go out of his way to make himself the easiest person in the world to like."

Hammond declared England's innings closed at 658 for eight, with Paynter unbeaten on 216. Stan McCabe contributed a magnificent 232 to Australia's reply of 411. The Aussies were forced to follow on but a century stand between Bill Brown (133) and Don Bradman (144) strangled England's victory chances, and Compo's first match against Australia ended in a draw.

He was trapped leg before by Tiger O'Reilly for six in the first innings of the second Test at Lord's, but even the perfectionist Hammond would have struggled to find fault with his unbeaten knock of seventy-six in the second innings that forced a draw just as the Aussies thought they had victory in their sights.

Mature performance

BILL O'REILLY: "We were even more impressed by Denis in the second Test at Lord's than at Trent Bridge. He played beautifully on a difficult pitch in the second innings just when we thought we were going to run through the England team. We had whipped five men out for seventy something, but Denis did not give us a sniff of a chance with a mature performance that helped save the match for England. We all knew that he was going to be a thorn in our side for years to come, but it was going to be enjoyable watching him because he was such an entertaining batsman."

Hat-trick heartbreak

DENIS COMPTON: "I have two outstanding memories of that Lord's Test. The first was watching our skipper Wally Hammond score a magnificent 240. It made me appreciate just what a master of the batting arts he was. I cannot recall him giving a single chance. He and Eddie Paynter put on 222 for the fourth wicket at much quicker than a run a minute and made the Australian attack look very ordinary. My other memory is not such a good one. I dropped Fleetwood-Smith at slip. It was a difficult chance that I would usually just have shrugged off. But if I had held it Essex fast bowler Ken Farnes would have had a hat-trick. He was tragically killed in the war when on a bombing mission as a pilot officer, and I often think about how my dropped catch robbed Ken of a place in the record books. Very sad."

Compo was selected for all five Tests that summer. The Old Trafford game was washed out, and it rained runs at the Oval in the final Test after the Aussies had clinched the series. This was the famous Hutton match in which the Yorkshire opener scored his world record 364 in a remarkable thirteen-hour marathon. The Compton contribution to the run riot was exactly one.

The £1 Test bet
DENIS COMPTON: "I sat in the stand with Eddie Paynter watching Len accumulate his enormous total. It was a magnificent innings, and it completely drained Len because of the concentration he gave to every single stroke. Eddie and I sat side by side in the pavilion watching him slowly grind the Aussie bowlers down. 'We're so numb from sitting that I bet you and I don't score ten between us,' said Eddie, who had been padded for hours on end. I could never resist a bet, and said, 'You're on. A pound that we get plenty between us.' That was the equivalent of a day's wages, remember, so we were both going to take the bet seriously. A few minutes later Eddie went in with the score at 546 for three. He did not trouble the scorer and returned after Tiger O'Reilly had got him leg before for nought. Then it was my turn and I managed just a single off Tiger before being

bowled in the next over by Mervyn Waite. I don't know who was more surprised, Mervyn or me. I trundled back to the pavilion, and handed a grinning Paynter his pound note."

Denis more than got his money back in free drinks. On every visit to Australia from then on he would get a call from Mervyn Waite. 'I owe you a drink,' was always his opening line. He and Denis would celebrate the fact that Compo was his only victim throughout his Test career. They always had reason to remember the Hutton Test when Len took an undeniable lead in his unofficial run race with Denis.

The Hutton versus Compton "war" was about to split the nation.

5: Hutton: The Truth

I just wish that I could have played the game
with the same carefree attitude as Denis.
Sir Leonard Hutton

THE cricketing careers of Denis Compton and Len Hutton ran parallel, and they came to epitomise the North versus South rivalry. Cricket supporters avidly followed their paths to glory run by run, boundary by boundary from when they first strode on to the stage in the mid-1930s as the new messiahs of the English game. They had tough acts to follow. Hobbs, Hammond, Hendren and Sutcliffe were heading for the sunset. Hutton and Compton represented the bright new dawn. Hutton took on the challenge with tenacious determination, Compton with panache and style. The nation hung on their every run, and such were their different approaches to the game and to life that the myth was perpetuated that they did not like each other.

A sneaking envy

SIR LEN HUTTON: "We were as different as chalk and cheese, but the truth of the matter is that I had a sneaking envy for the way Denis played the game. If anything, I was the prisoner of my technique while Denis had this in-born ability just to play it off the cuff. As for that business about us not liking each other, I can show you telephone bills to prove that is nonsense. Hardly a week goes by without us talking to each other on the telephone, remembering the old days and discussing the modern game. It's true we did not socialise that much when we were playing but, like our cricket, we did things differently. If I have one regret, it's that

I was not able to play the game with the carefree attitude that Denis always showed. He got so much enjoyment out of batting, while many of the rest of us often found it something of a hardship."

I got this extraordinary confession from Sir Len while compiling material for the *This Is Your Life* tribute to Denis in 1987. We talked at his Surrey home where he became quite nervous when trusted with the secret of the *Life* programme. He was concerned that he would let something slip during his regular telephone chats with Denis, and for the three weeks leading up to the show he found excuses not to talk to his old pal. He was not in the best of health, and rather than go to the studio he filmed his contribution to the programme. I asked both Sir Len and Denis for their memories of each other ...

Hutton c & b Compton
SIR LEN HUTTON: "The Yorkshire spectators could be quite vociferous against Denis, but that was just their way of supporting me. Deep down, I know that like me they had great respect and admiration for the way Denis could play the game and they were always warm with their applause when he scored runs at Headingley. I remember a magnificent catch he made off his own bowling during that summer of 1947 when it was his batting that was making all the headlines. He threw himself to the left and held the ball one handed. I was the batsman on the receiving end when playing for Yorkshire against Middlesex at Lord's, and I had been convinced the ball was on the way to the boundary. I often remind Denis of that wonderful piece of cricket, but always add that he should not forget that I once bowled him."

Compton b Hutton
DENIS COMPTON: "I was playing for the MCC in the season curtain raiser against Yorkshire at Lord's on May Day 1937.

The reason I know the exact date is that Len is always reminding me! I had rattled up forty-odd runs when Len was put on with his crafty leg spin. I cracked his first ball for four and went down the wicket to repeat the shot off his next ball. It was Len's wrong 'un and it bowled me all ends up. I could talk about Len Hutton all day. He was the greatest English batsman of our generation, and only Peter May has surpassed him in my estimation. We always had the deepest admiration and respect for each other, and it is a complete myth that we did not like each other. Mind you, the Yorkshire public seemed in two minds about me. They considered me a bit flash - 'a typical bloody Southerner'. I recall playing for Middlesex against Yorkshire in Sheffield once when a stray dog ran on the field. As I fielded it the little what's it bit my hand and I had to go off for treatment. The Yorkshire folk loved that, and I was treated to shouts of, 'Put some Brylcreem on it' ... and ... 'It's taken our Len weeks to train the dog to do that.' To be honest, I enjoyed the Yorkshire fans and their humour. It was the nearest you could get in England to the ear-bashing you got from the jokers on the famous Sydney Hill. The Yorkshire spectators really knew their cricket and were always quick to appreciate it when I made runs. But woe betide me whenever I dropped a catch or played a silly shot! They really got behind Len, and I admired them for their loyalty."

Skeleton from the cupboard

SIR LEN HUTTON: "Everybody knows that Denis had the reputation for running out partners, and I have to admit that I had to concentrate that much harder when batting with him because he was so unpredictable. He never ran me out, but here's a skeleton from my cupboard. I once ran Denis out! We were playing the West Indies at the Oval in 1950, and Denis was going nicely on forty-four when he called for a sharpish single. I sent him back. A quick throw removed the bails and he was run out. We could have made the run if

I had gone for it, and I felt terrible but it was typical of Denis that he just shrugged and accepted it without holding any sort of grudge. In reverse circumstances I would have wanted to murder him! That was the innings in which I carried my bat for 202. Denis was the next top scorer, and might easily have gone on to a century but for my in-built caution. I should have gone for that run. Even now, during our many chats on the telephone, I still apologise to him, and he just laughs and says, 'You always were an old run miser.' Denis and I enemies? Don't you believe a word of it."

The dropped bat
DENIS COMPTON: There was another time when I should have been run out when batting with Len. It was against Don Bradman's 1948 Australians at the Oval, The Don's famous last match in which he was bowled for a duck by Eric Hollies when needing just four runs for a perfect average of one hundred. We were shot out in our first innings for fifty-two, of which Len scored thirty. I was going for a comfortable single with Len when I dropped my bat. Lindsay Hassett had the ball in his hand and could easily have knocked down my stumps. But he saw that I was fumbling to pick up my bat and declined to throw. That's the sort of sportsmanship that was around in those days. It was a time when batsmen walked without waiting for the umpire. It's the type of fair-play approach that sadly seems to be going out of the game."

The betting man
SIR LEN HUTTON: "When I think of Denis I have to say that gambling always comes to mind. While I would wear blinkers in the dressing-room thinking of the next run, he would be on the telephone placing a bet or at the card table playing for high stakes. I played with him during a rain interruption in his first Test against New Zealand and quickly realised that I was best off not taking him on at cards. He was quite

reckless with his cash, and it did not seem to bother him at all whether he won or lost. I wanted to win at everything, and Denis and I used to have some rare old ding dongs on the tennis court when we used to play for half-a-crown. Even at that game he used to come up with some amazing strokes of his own invention. He could also conjure up unbelievable shots on the golf course where he was, to say the very least, unpredictable."

A sense of humour
DENIS COMPTON: "Len was so preoccupied with his captaincy and his batting that people never really got to appreciate that he had a great sense of humour. I recall the 1953 Ashes Test at Lord's when we were together facing Lindwall and Miller bowling flat out. They were as deadly as I had ever known them and you could have cut the tension with a knife. After one particularly hostile over from Lindwall, Len summoned me. As I walked down the wicket to meet him I thought that as skipper he was going to talk about tactics, and I'm sure that's what everybody watching thought. What he actually said was, 'We must be mad, Denis. There must be easier ways to make a living than this!'"

No hoorays for Hollywood
SIR LEN HUTTON: "There was only one time that I remember when Denis showed any obvious annoyance with me. We had stopped off in Hawaii on our way back from the 1950-1 tour to Australia during which Denis had been vice-captain and had had a wretched run of luck with the bat. A telegram arrived for Denis from the British actor Nigel Bruce in Hollywood. It was an invitation for us to spend three days in California as guests of the Hollywood Actors' Cricket Club. They wanted us to play a one-day game and then see the sights. Denis could not believe it when I said I would rather head straight for home. We had a team vote, and there was a slight majority to give Hollywood a miss. Denis was

devastated. I think that summed up the difference between us. He always loved the bright lights, while I preferred a quieter life. Thinking back on it, I now wish I had voted to go to Hollywood!"

Clowning at the Palladium

DENIS COMPTON: "Nigel Bruce, who was the most famous of all the Watsons opposite Basil Rathbone in the Sherlock Holmes films, was one of dozens of stage and screen celebrities that I got to know through cricket. I have to admit that I went into something of a sulk over having to turn down that trip of a lifetime to Hollywood. I was particularly looking forward to meeting up again with C. Aubrey Smith, who founded the Hollywood Cricket Club. Danny Kaye was also going to play against us. We had clowned around at the Palladium during one of his visits, and he had got me up on stage to show him how cricket should be played. Danny then took the bat and had the audience roaring with laughter with an hilarious mime of a batsman at the wicket. He was a comic genius. A particularly good friend of mine was that great British actor Trevor Howard, who used to have it written into his film contracts that he must be given time off to watch the Test matches at Lord's and the Oval. For years we had a routine in which he would telephone me and say in that distinctive voice of his, 'I'm here and a drink is waiting.' That was the signal for me to meet him in the saloon bar of my local village pub, the Black Horse, in Fulmer. Trevor knew his cricket inside out and back to front, and would have swapped all his leading roles for the chance to open the England innings against Australia at Lord's."

In 1984 I compiled a *Cricket Heroes* book in collaboration with my old friend Eric Morecambe, who was into his third term as President of the Lord's Taverners. Eric arranged for me to interview Trevor Howard for a contribution to the book. We talked while he was dressed as a medieval knight on the set of *Sword of the Valiant* in which he was starring with Sean Connery.

An art form
TREVOR HOWARD: "I would much rather have a cricket bat in my hand than a sword. Just think what damage Denis Compton could have wreaked with a flashing broadsword. He would have been a champion swordsman for King Arthur's knights. They would have all fallen to his late cuts! For me, cricket is an art form. And there was no better artist than Denis Compton. The cricket pitch was his canvas, and he painted wonderful scenes that remained in the memory of all those lucky enough to see his magical strokes. I was a keen follower of both Denis and Len Hutton, and I would say that they gave me more pleasure than just about anybody else on this earth. They were vastly different in their approach to the game, but the end product from each of them was both masterly and memorable. I never went along with the Hutton versus Compton nonsense. We spectators were lucky to have them both at their peak together, and I always considered it a privilege to watch each of them at work. A Compton sweep ... a Hutton drive ... a pint at the Tavern ... what more could a man want? To use an analogy from the film world, they were co-stars sharing the lead role. Both were scene stealers, and both were worth the price of admission on their own. For me, it was never Hutton against Compton, but Hutton *and* Compton."

Going down the wicket
SIR LEN HUTTON: "My abiding memory of Denis is of him literally jumping out of his crease to take on the left-arm spin of Ernie Toshack. It was in the fourth Test in Adelaide in 1947 when Denis became only the third Englishman to complete two centuries in a Test. The Australian crowd roared every time Denis advanced down the wicket. It was great entertainment, although I don't think Ernie enjoyed it

very much. To this day I have never seen anybody to match Denis for going down the wicket to spinners. It took great nerve, inventive batting skill and a wonderful eye. I would never have dared to play that way. That was Denis. He had such a sense of adventure and fun."

Mobbed by the girls

DENIS COMPTON: "What I remember of that Adelaide Test is that I played with a torn shirt. My memory is not playing tricks when I say that we used to get mobbed by young Australian girls on the way to the wicket. They treated us a little like pop stars are treated today. One of the girls ripped my shirt and I was going so well in that match that I refused to change it – one of my little superstitions. As I was returning to the middle after the tea interval my batting partner Joe 'The Joker' Hardstaff was walking beside me. Suddenly he dropped back a pace, put a finger in the tear and dragged it so that it was suddenly a gaping hole. 'Remind me not to put that shirt on any of my horses,' Keith Miller said to me as I arrived at the crease. Both Arthur Morris and I scored hundreds in each innings, which was the first time that had ever happened in a Test."

Len Hutton was appointed the first professional captain of England this century, and in 1953-4 he led a squad including Compo on a headline-hitting tour of the West Indies. The Third Test in Georgetown has become known in the cricket history books as the "Test of the Flying Bottles".

The angry crowd

SIR LEN HUTTON: "We had a little, uh, local difficulty in Georgetown. The crowd rioted after Peter May had clearly run out Clifford McWatt as he was scampering to try to complete a century partnership with John Holt. There was no doubt that he was out, but many of the spectators went wild. As captain, I decided to call the players to the middle, out of range of the hundreds of bottles that were being hurled towards us by the angriest crowd I had ever seen. It was really quite frightening, but it was typical of Denis that he could see the funny side. He and Johnny Wardle helped ease the tension by picking up rum bottles and pretending to drain them and then staggering as if drunk. Thank goodness, the crowd reacted in similar good humour otherwise it could have got very nasty."

A tough character

DENIS COMPTON: "Len showed just what a tough character he was during that riot. One of the West Indian umpires suggested that it would be wisest to leave the field. Len's reply was pure Yorkshire, 'We'll stay. We want a couple more wickets tonight!' He somehow managed to keep his temper and his discipline during a series when we were subjected to a procession of diabolical umpiring decisions. For instance, in the second Test I was given out leg before when stretching forward to a googly! Fred Trueman was a youngster on the trip, and was continually in hot water with his fellow Yorkshireman because of the way he let his emotions show on the pitch. It was not exactly the expected behaviour of an England cricketer, and I am sure that when Freddie got an older and wiser head on his shoulders he would have admitted he was wrong to have reacted the way he did in very trying circumstances."

Fiery Fred could not win on that tour. It was reported that he had insulted an umpire during the fourth Test at Port-of-Spain, but on this occasion he was a victim of mistaken identity.

Innocent bystander

DENIS COMPTON: "Freddie was an innocent bystander. It was Tom Graveney, of all people, who upset the umpire. I took the ball for the last over before lunch in the fourth Test at Port-of-Spain. I bowled to John Holt, who had survived a series of what we thought were wrong umpiring calls. My final ball was a googly that Holt clearly edged into the safe hands of Tom at second slip. Tom pocketed the ball and started to walk back to the pavilion for lunch. But there was no sign of movement from either Holt or the umpire's finger. 'That's the fourth blankety-blank time,' said the usually placid Graveney, who threw the ball to the ground in anger. The crowd booed and jeered, and Len rollicked Tom for his understandable reaction. It was a very difficult tour, and Len came through it magnificently. He scored 205 in the final Test to steer us to a nine-wicket victory to square the series. It was the first double century by an England captain in an overseas Test, and was an innings full of guts and character that typified what a great battler Len was."

A stand to remember

SIR LEN HUTTON: "Funnily enough, considering how many times we played in the same Test team, Denis and I did not have too many stands together. We managed a century stand in the first Test against New Zealand in 1949, but the only other one that sticks in my mind is the 248 partnership against the West Indies at Lord's in 1939. We were only together for 140 minutes, and, surprisingly, I managed to outscore Denis against a West Indies attack that included Manny Martindale, Leslie Hylton and a veteran Learie Constantine. The odd thing about that series is that eight-ball overs were bowled as an experiment, and I found that it called for a different approach. I was being quite cautious about my batting until Denis joined me with that jaunty walk of his. He immediately started going for the runs, and I took the lead from him. It was very enjoyable if a little reckless."

Commando course accident

DENIS COMPTON: "Len had scored a slow, chanceless ninety-one by the time I joined him. The sight of me coming to the wicket seemed to act like an electric shock. He hit twenty-one fours to my sixteen as we peppered the boundaries. Those were the days when Len used to hook, a stroke that he dropped from his game after his wartime accident on a commando course. He had such a bad fracture of his left arm that it shortened by two inches. The chilling thing I recall from that stand of ours at Lord's is that while we were coming out after the tea interval a public announcement was being made to the effect that volunteers were required for National Service."

Hutton and Compton were about to have five peak years taken from their cricketing careers by wartime call-ups. Their Test career batting averages were remarkably similar:

Hutton: 79 Tests, 138 innings, 15 n.o., 6,971 runs, 19 100s, 56.67av
Compton: 78 Tests, 131 innings, 15 n.o., 5,807 runs, 17 100s, 50.06av

How would theses statistics have read without the interruption of the war during which Denis lost not only the chance to add to his Test cap collection but the opportunity to play football for England?

And that is who we are going to meet next: Denis Compton the footballer.

6: The Footballer

If Denis had given all his attention to football
he would have challenged even Tom Finney
for his England shirt
Joe Mercer

IT will come as a surprise to many football fans that "the other" Denis Compton - the footballer - played only fifty-four League games for Arsenal, the club with which he spent his entire career. And here's a question that will stump even most collectors of sporting trivia: "At which ground did Denis Compton play most of his home first-team matches?" If you say Highbury, you will be wrong. The answer is White Hart Lane. Denis played more wartime than peacetime matches for Arsenal, who shared Tottenham's ground during the war because Highbury was being used as an air raid precaution centre. Another little-publicised fact is that Denis nearly became a Glasgow Rangers player ...

Rangers make an offer
DENIS COMPTON: "George Allison, who took over as Arsenal manager following the sudden death of Herbert Chapman, called me into his office after we had played a friendly against Rangers in the annual curtain-raiser to the 1936-7 season. 'I won't beat about the bush, Compton,' he said in his gravelly voice. 'The Rangers management were so impressed with you that they would like to sign you. They have mentioned a fee of two thousand pounds. I feel duty bound to tell you this, although we see you as part of our family here at Arsenal. The decision to go or stay is yours.' I did not have to give it a second's thought. Arsenal was the only club in the world that I wanted to play for. Mr. Allison

was delighted, and rewarded me by selecting me for my debut against Derby County at Highbury the following Saturday."

In keeping with his storybook career, Denis scored the first Arsenal goal in a 2–2 draw with Derby County in front of a crowd of 65,000 – most of them standing on the Highbury terraces that Denis had been sweeping for the previous four years as a groundstaff boy. It was one of fifteen First Division goals that he scored for Arsenal spread over a span of fourteen years, and not including those netted during the years lost to the war. His contemporaries claim that he had just two faults that prevented him from becoming an exceptional rather than just a very good left winger: one, that he did not release the ball quickly enough; two, that he was very much one-footed.

One-footed magician
LES COMPTON: "From his youngest days playing for fun in Alexandra Road kick-abouts, Denis was completely one-footed. He used his right just to stand on and did almost everything with the left foot. Even so, he could almost make the ball sit up and talk and used to run rings round me. I concentrated on power and made the most of my physical strength, while Denis perfected his ball skill and deceptive acceleration. He was a born dribbler, all done with his left foot. It brought him a lot of success with Hampstead Town and then Nunhead in the Isthmian League, but he found a big difference when he joined the Highbury groundstaff. Arsenal did their best to make him a two-footed player, and they used to make him wear a slipper on his left foot in training to encourage him to kick it with his right. It used to work until he got into a proper match, and then he would instinctively go back to working almost exclusively with his left foot. But what a left foot. It was magical, just like his cricket bat."

Ted Drake was the legendary battering-ram of a centre–forward at Arsenal when Denis was starting out on his football career. They became close friends, mainly because of a shared love for cricket. Ted, who once scored a First Division record seven goals with eight shots for Arsenal at Aston Villa, fitted in a handful of County matches with Hampshire but was first to admit that he was not in Compo's league as a batsman. They played several First Division matches together, but most of their football was confined to the wartime league. When managing the Chelsea team that won the League Championship in 1954-5, Ted was always happy to find time to talk about cricket.

Beating one man too many

TED DRAKE: "The only fault that Denis had as a footballer was that he always wanted to beat one man too many. I would be waiting in the middle for his cross while he was busy enjoying himself out on the wing trying to dribble past everybody in sight. He was such a lovely boy that you could not bawl him out, but I know our manager George Allison and trainer Tom Whittaker used to give him lots of lectures about releasing the ball. There were few who could match his skill, and he would have been up there with Matthews and Finney if only he could have disciplined himself into making an earlier pass. We got along famously because, like Denis, I loved my cricket as much as football. I recall a testimonial cricket match played at Highbury for Denis when we went in to bat wearing Arsenal shirts and scored more than two hundred runs in under an hour! The ball spent more time in the Highbury stands and on the terraces than on the pitch. Denis was a real charmer, and always went out of his way to get me tickets for matches at Lord's when I was manager at Chelsea. He used to come and watch us play at Stamford Bridge, and I told him that if it was not for his wonky knee I would have him playing on our left wing. Mind you, he would have been under orders to release the ball!"

Dribbling for fun

DENIS COMPTON: "It's true that I used to hog the ball. I couldn't help it. I think it was a habit that went back to my schoolboy days when I used to keep a tennis ball at my feet for hours on end. Using my left foot just came naturally to me, and I found dribbling a lot of fun. I just wonder what my approach to football might have been had the money existed in the game that there is today. Cricket was always my first love, with football an added bonus that made the winters pass quicker. The most I earned a week as a footballer was £14 plus a £2 bonus if we won. I did not even reach the dizzy heights of the £20 maximum wage that was introduced after I retired. When you think of the crowds we were drawing – rarely less than 50,000 – it makes you realise why some of the great players of the era were very bitter about what they were paid. One game I remember in particular was against Charlton at The Valley in 1937. Alex James, my all-time hero, was recalled for one of his final games and he played alongside me. Mr. James, as I called him, said to me, 'These are the tactics: when I get the ball start running straight down that touchline. Don't look for me. I'll find you.' He did not miss me with a pass all afternoon. His appearance in the team drew a crowd of 77,000 to The Valley, but like the rest of us all that Alex James earned was £8, which was the pre-war maximum wage. I suppose that today I would have had to elect to play football for a living purely on economic grounds. That would have meant no cricket career. It just does not bear thinking about. I enjoyed my football, but I just cannot imagine a life without cricket. I never became wealthy playing cricket or football, but I have many rich memories that money could not buy."

The peak years for Compton the footballer came during the war. He played 126 matches for Arsenal and scored 74 goals, helping Arsenal win the Regional League three times and playing a creative role in a 7–1 crushing of Charlton Athletic in the Football League South Cup Final at Wembley in 1943. He was selected to play for the England international team in fourteen matches, often in a star-studded forward line that read: Stanley Matthews, Raich Carter, Tommy Lawton, Jimmy Hagan and Compton. His Arsenal clubmate Laurie Scott sometimes supported him from defence ...

Oh, what a lovely black eye

LAURIE SCOTT, a quick as lightning Yorkshireman who played in England's first seventeen international matches immediately after the war, was deeply distressed when Denis died on what was Laurie's eightieth birthday. He talked as warmly about him as if he had lost a member of his family: "Denis was an absolutely marvellous character, who never got too big for his boots despite all his success. We played football together for Arsenal and also for England during the war. When I first came down to London from Bradford in the 1930s I lived in digs. I hadn't been married long and when my wife joined me Denis's mum and dad, Harry and Jessie, took us both under their wing. They really couldn't have been kinder. Denis and his brother Leslie were contrasting personalities and very different in style on the pitch. Leslie was all strength and dependability and a real powerhouse in the air with his headed clearances. Denis was all slippery skill and speed, and extremely unpredictable. He and I appeared in a couple of wartime internationals together. Denis had a stormer in the 8–0 defeat over Scotland at Maine Road in 1944, and then we played together in the Victory International at Hampden Park when the Scots won 2–1. He was an extremely skilful player but he didn't have much of a right foot, and I noted as a full-back that he went on the outside all the time. We were direct opponents in only one major match, a game played for the Red Cross between the RAF and the Army at Wembley. I was at right-back for the RAF, Denis at outside-left for the Army. We had a bit of a laugh and a banter together in the tunnel waiting to come out to be introduced to the Deputy Prime Minister Clement Attlee. But we were deadly serious about what was a very competitive game with a lot of pride and prestige at stake. I found that Denis was extremely tough to knock off the ball unless you timed your tackle perfectly. He not only had good ball control but was immensely strong. If you tried to lean on him you would bounce off and fall over. My main memory of the match is going up with him to challenge for a high ball. We collided and I ended up with a black eye. Given a shiner by the great Denis Compton! I was very proud of that bruise."

If there was a better centre-forward around than Ted Drake, then it was Tommy Lawton, whose peak years collided with the war, during which he regularly wore the number nine England shirt. Tommy was the "Head Master" of football who could power the ball with his head harder than many could kick it. I once conducted a poll in the *Daily Express* inviting readers to vote for England's greatest centre-forward. Tommy, who won by a runaway margin, telephoned me to say: "The readers have got it wrong. I'm very flattered, but Dixie Dean should have come out on top." Tommy scored 23 goals in 22 full internationals, plus another 25 in wartime internationals when many of his goals came following centres from either Stanley Matthews on the right wing or Compo on the left.

Eight-goal wonders
TOMMY LAWTON: "Denis was a wonderful crosser of a ball with his left foot, and set up many goals for me. His centres often deceived the goalkeeper because he would put so much swerve on the ball. 'You're crossing leg breaks,' I once told him. He was almost as clever a dribbler as Stanley Matthews. I can give him no higher praise. If it had not been for the war, he would have won a pile of official England caps. I remember us putting eight goals past Wales and then

another eight past Scotland in 1943, and I reckon Denis laid on at least five of them with his great individual work out on the left wing. With Stanley out wide on the right and Denis doing his tricks on the left, all I had to do was make sure I gave my centre-half the slip and then get into position for what were always accurate crosses. Denis was a delightful man off the pitch, quieter than I expected but very jolly in the bar. I lost quite a few bob to him at the card table, and he could throw a nifty dart. He was the envy of the England team because of the way he drew the interest of the ladies. They were always chasing him, but Denis was newly married when I knew him in those war years and he usually managed to behave himself despite all the temptations. It could not have been easy for him because he was such a good-looking chap."

I spent all of the 1960s and into the 1970s as a football reporter, first for the *Daily Herald* (which became the *Sun* in 1964), and then the *Daily Express*. I was always mixing with former players who had Denis Compton stories to tell, often with Denis quietly listening and nodding, smiling and sometimes adding to the yarns that raided his treasure chest of memories. One of my favourite press-box colleagues was Joe Hulme, who had been the Compton of his time as a footballer and cricketer. He became a familiar figure at football and cricket grounds as a sports gossip writer for the *Sunday People*. Like Denis, he played cricket for Middlesex and football for Arsenal.

Key man for Arsenal
JOE HULME: "Denis was always ready to listen to older professionals, and was very respectful. Patsy Hendren gave him a lot of batting tips, and he used to seek both of us out for advice on how best to combine football and cricket. Denis would have made a bigger impact at Arsenal before the war but for Cliff Bastin still producing peak performances. It

meant he had to spend a lot of time in the reserves. He played his best football during the war years, and was a key man in the Arsenal team that threatened to dominate the wartime Southern League. Nothing seemed to phase Denis. He had a great temperament, and was a really cool character when it came to taking vital penalties. Mind you, he was a bit nervy before a match and used to like to puff on a cigarette to steady his nerves. This meant nipping into the toilet because smoking was forbidden in the Arsenal dressing-room. I played few football matches with Denis, but got to know him well when I switched to sports reporting. He was always good for a bit of gossip, and used to telephone me with horse racing tips. He was a devil for the gee-gees, and spent much more time reading the *Sporting Life* than any cricket or football coaching manuals."

Superstitions

LES COMPTON: "Both Denis and I were very superstitious, and we would always follow the same routine in the dressing-room before going out to bat or to play football. When batting, Denis always put his right pad on first and his right glove before his left, and he used to insist on his partner going through the gate first when leaving the pavilion at the start of a session. Another thing, he insisted on his partner walking on the right side, and we joked with him that he wanted to show his best side to the photographers. In the football dressing-room he would studiously kick a ball against the radiator pipes at Arsenal, always the exact same number of times. My big superstition was that I always had to be the last man to leave the dressing-room, whether going out to field or to play for Arsenal. It took some getting used to for me when I was made Arsenal captain and had to lead the team out during the wartime games. I used to let everybody file out past me, and then chase to the front just before we went out on to the pitch. I remember that on the morning of our first FA Cup tie in 1950 I cleaned our windows.

We won the match, and so every Cup match morning I followed the same routine and we went all the way to Wembley. We had the cleanest windows in town!"

Palladium act
TED DRAKE: "But for the outbreak of war, Denis might have become a London Palladium star. He was one of six of us at Arsenal who auditioned at the Palladium with a head-tennis act. Cliff Bastin, George Male, Eddie Hapgood, Denis, his brother Les and I worked out a routine in training in which we mixed ball juggling with heading. George Black, the Palladium impresario, read a report about it in a newspaper and invited us along to test it out on stage. He was sufficiently impressed to offer us £100 a week between us for a down-the-bill act, and added that he would also get us regular work at the Butlin's Holiday Camps. He reckoned that would earn us another £50 a week for the pool. This, remember, when we were all on just £8 a week wages. Then along came Hitler and wrecked the plan before we could launch our stage act."

In 1939, Compo appeared with his Arsenal team-mates in the film thriller *The Arsenal Stadium Mystery*. It involved the poisoning of a footballer during a match in which Arsenal played Brentford. Bernard Joy, my old press-box colleague who was an esteemed football columnist with the London *Star* and then *Evening Standard*, played in the match three years after becoming the last amateur to be capped by England

Magnetic attraction
BERNARD JOY: "We took some terrible ribbing from the fans, particularly when playing away, after appearing in the film. Denis was easily the most photogenic of all the players. The director kept calling for close-ups of him, and it was Denis who was selected to pose for publicity photographs with the attractive female lead Greta Gynt. He had an almost

73

magnetic attraction for the ladies, but never used to flaunt it. Until George Best came along, few players have drawn as many female spectators to sporting events. They filmed an actual Arsenal match against Brentford to feature in the film, and all the players were paid £50 a week in bonuses during the three-week making of the film. We told Denis that the real mystery was why a Hollywood agent had not signed him up. Actually, the alleged acting of all the players, including Denis, was more wooden than the goalposts!"

Dramatic equaliser

EDDIE HAPGOOD, England and Arsenal captain in the 1930s, took Compo under his wing and advised him how to take on full-backs ... of which he was one of the very best: "I remember a wartime game at Brighton when Denis arrived at the last minute on the back of an Army motorbike. He went out on to the pitch in borrowed boots and played a blinder. He scored a couple of goals, including one from the penalty spot and a rare one with his right foot. He could hardly keep his eyes open in the dressing-room afterwards, and told us that he had come straight from a five-hour weapons-training session at Aldershot. His hands were still oily from dismantling and putting together Bren guns. In the 1941 Cup Final against Preston at Wembley, Les Compton smacked an early penalty against a post and Denis scored a dramatic equaliser to force a 1–1 draw. There was always something happening when the Comptons were around."

A living legend

BILL SHANKLY, larger-than-life idol of the Kop, cuddled Compo like a long-lost brother when he met him at Highbury after Liverpool had played a League game against Arsenal in the late 1960s. I was among a posse of pressmen witnessing their reunion. Liverpool manager Shanks told us in that distinctive bagpipes accent of his: "This man is a legend in his own lifetime, but in the wrong sport. I played against him many times during the war years when he was at his absolute peak. He could have been a great, great footballer, but decided to concentrate instead on that silly game called cricket. That's a game for girls. Football's a man's game, and Denis Compton was a man's man. It's not something I talk about too often because the memory makes me go dizzy, but I played against Denis when England beat Scotland 8–0. And we were lucky that day to get nil. Denis and that tormentor Stanley Matthews ran rings round our defence. I was playing at wing-half with Matt Busby, and we both agreed that on that day Denis was every bit as good as the great Matthews. Not too many wingers have had that said about them. The fact that he gave so much of his time and energy to cricket was a criminal waste of his football talent. He was very nearly in the Tom Finney class, and as I reckon Tom was the greatest thing on two feet it shows you just how highly I rated this man. They tell me he was a genius of a cricketer, but I'm no expert on that. To me, cricket is something that gets in the way when I'm waiting for the football season to start. I just know from the wartime matches that I played against Denis that he could have been as big in football as he was in cricket. We played together in a wartime representative game at Aldershot when he beat five men before scoring with a scorcher of a cross-shot. As I congratulated him I said, 'Throw away the cricket bat, Denis, and concentrate on football.'"

Good Old Big Head

DENIS COMPTON: "Some of those wartime matches were just crazy. I recall that my brother Les played in goal one week for Arsenal and at centre-forward the next when he scored ten goals in a 15–2 victory over Clapton Orient. Six of the goals came from his head, and on the strength of that performance he was selected at centre-forward in a wartime international against Wales. Then, a year or so later, he was picked at left-back. Talk about versatile! I was very proud of

75

Leslie's football achievements. He did not win a regular place in the Arsenal League team until after the war and, at thirty-eight in 1950, became the oldest player ever to make his England debut. The fans at Highbury used to call him affectionately 'Good Old Big Head' because he was just about unbeatable in the air."

The delayed medal

LES COMPTON: "I was proud to be made Arsenal club captain during the war, but when manager Tom Whittaker brought Joe Mercer to Highbury in 1946 I tossed the ball to him in the dressing-room and said, 'You're the man to lead us, Joe.' I had discussed it with Denis, and we both agreed that Joe was the right man to captain the team. His leadership was vital in helping us win the League title in 1948, and both Denis and I had Football Championship medals to go with the County Championship medals we had won the previous summer with Middlesex. Denis had to wait until the following season to get his medal. He had played only fourteen first-team games because of cricket commitments and injuries, but it was decided that in future anybody who played a minimum fourteen games should qualify for a medal. We were as proud as punch to play together in the 1950 FA Cup Final, and to go up the Wembley steps to collect our medals was just unforgettable."

Joe Mercer, who became football's favourite "Uncle" figure, joined Arsenal from Everton immediately after the war, having been written off as finished by the Merseyside club following a string of knee operations. He of the bandy legs and banana-size smile, became an instant hero at Highbury. Joe was particularly fond of the Compton brothers.

Defying the skipper

JOE MERCER: "Both Denis and Leslie were an absolute joy to play with. Les was all heart and head. There have been few to match him for heading a ball. As for Denis, he was as natural a footballer as he was a cricketer. If he had been able to give all his attention to playing football I reckon he would have challenged even the great Tom Finney for the England number eleven shirt. There was the famous incident in the 1950 FA Cup semi-final against Chelsea at White Hart Lane in which the Compton brothers showed the value of their radar understanding. We were trailing 2–1 with thirteen minutes to go when Denis forced a corner on the left. He waved for his brother to get into the penalty area, but I said to Les, 'Oi, I'm the captain and I'm telling you to stay back here in defence.' Les decided to defy me, and I was fuming as he ran upfield. He arrived on the edge of the penalty area just as Denis took the corner. The ball found Good Old Big Head, and he powered the ball into the net for an equaliser. I was the first to reach him to pat him on the back. 'In future, Big Head,' I said, 'ignore everything I say.' Of course, we won the replay and went to Wembley for the final against Liverpool. What a proud day that was for the Comptons."

The brandy snap

DENIS COMPTON: "I decided that the FA Cup Final would be the last game of my football career. My knee would no longer stand the strain of playing a season of football on top of the County and Test cricket. I badly wanted to go out a winner, but the way I played in the first-half against Liverpool I think I would have been pulled off if substitutes had been allowed. I was a stone or so overweight for football at around thirteen and a half stone, and I was quickly out of puff. Manager Tom Whittaker knew I was struggling, and gave me a good pep talk at half-time. 'This is the last forty-five minutes of your career,' he said. 'Go out there and make every one of them count. Go out a winner.' My old idol Alex James, who was helping out in the dressing-room, called me into the bath area. 'Get this down you,' he whispered, handing me a small glass of liquid. I looked at it, smelt it and pulled a face. It was brandy. I decided that Alex had been around in the game long enough to know what he was doing, and so I drank the brandy in one go. Whether it was psychological or what I don't know, but it certainly put the snap back in my game in the second-half and I felt quite pleased with my contribution to our 2–0 victory."

Compo collected his FA Cup winner's medal from the Queen, shook hands with George VI, and no doubt reflected that few players had walked up the Wembley steps a winner after so few first-team appearances.

I can think of no other player who has League Championship and FA Cup winner's medals to show for a full career stretching to just fifty-four League games and a handful of Cup ties. Denis played one more match the following week against League leaders Portsmouth at Highbury where the FA Cup was on display, and then – concerned by his weight and an increasingly troublesome knee – bowed out of football.

Denis stood 5 foot 11inches tall, and his best playing weight for football was around 12 stone. By the time he hung up his boots he had ballooned close to 14 stone, and he was no longer able to race past full-backs as in his slimline days.

Compo would certainly have made a much bigger impact as a footballer but for the war robbing him of the best years of his footballing life.

7: Compo at War

*For thousands like me, Denis
was a shining light during
the bleak years of the war*
Benny Green

WHEN war was declared on 3 September 1939, Denis was twenty-one and just establishing himself as a dual force in the worlds of cricket and football. He had become a key batsman for the England and Middlesex cricket teams, and was about to challenge the legendary Highbury hero Cliff "Boy" Bastin, for the regular number eleven Arsenal shirt. The world was at his feet when he and big brother Leslie reported to Highbury for training that late summer of 1939.

"We are at war ..."
LES COMPTON: "Denis and I went to Highbury to train with the reserves. The first team had played three First Division matches and we were both hopeful of making the breakthrough for regular places in the League side. We were later reporting back than the other fifty-two professionals on the staff because of our commitments to Middlesex. Then Neville Chamberlain made his 'We are at war with Germany' speech on the wireless, and from then on our lives were turned upside down. All our contracts at Arsenal were suspended, and the League programme abandoned."

Special Constable
DENIS COMPTON: "Of course it was shattering, but everybody was in the same boat. The attitude throughout

the country was, 'Let's get this war over and get back to normal as quickly as possible.' Les and I became Special Constables for a few months while waited for our call-up papers. We looked like something out of the Keystone Kops in our police uniforms and helmets. I soon got my call-up papers and joined an anti-aircraft regiment of the Royal Artillery based at East Grinstead. I was a very square peg in a very round hole. Then the Army had the bright idea of making serving sportsmen physical training instructors, and I was transferred to Aldershot for training and became a sergeant instructor. All the time I was managing to get time off to play in weekend matches, often at White Hart Lane where Arsenal staged their wartime League and Cup games. That was really strange, playing at Tottenham, the club that had traditionally been looked on by Arsenal supporters as 'the enemy'."

Denis made what was his last "live" appearance in a television studio in February 1996 when he came on as a surprise *This Is Your Life* guest for multi-talented jazz musician/critic, cricket historian, broadcaster and writer Benny Green. I scripted the show, and a major highlight for both Benny and me was to sit down with Denis after the programme and listen to him reminiscing about his own life and times. Denis had not long before had a hip replacement and was not in the best of health, but the sparkle came back into his eyes and the years seemed to fall away from him as Benny got him talking about those war years.

A shining light
BENNY GREEN: "It would seem depressing us talking about the war, but the point I was making to Denis during our conversation was that he brought a shining light to those bleak years for thousands like me. He was a hero for all seasons. I can recall as clearly as anything watching him winning matches on his own with amazing trickery down

the wing. If television cameras had been there to capture one goal against Queen's Park Rangers, they would still be showing it now as one of the goals of the century. He waltzed past four or five defenders with a dribbling run down the left wing, and then cut inside and beat the goalkeeper with a swerving shot. It was real *Roy of the Rovers* stuff. In another game he was on the same pitch as the wizard of wingers, Stanley Matthews. It was the South champions against the North champions wartime League final at Stamford Bridge. Denis was on the left wing for Arsenal and Stanley was guesting on the right for Blackpool, although still officially on Stoke City's books at the time. Denis ran Blackpool's defence inside out in the first half and created two goals to give Arsenal a 2-0 lead. Then Matthews took over and handed out similar treatment to the Arsenal defence to set up a 4–2 victory in a classic game. On that day Denis had looked every bit as good a winger as the great Matthews."

Matthews, The Master

DENIS COMPTON: "I would not want to spoil Benny's memory, but to be honest it is nonsense to mention me in the same breath as Stanley Matthews. He was to football what Jack Hobbs was to cricket: The Master. I had the thrill of playing with him several times in wartime internationals and exhibition games and can state quite categorically that there was nobody to touch him for ball control and dribbling skill. There was a game against Scotland at Maine Road when they included players of the calibre of Matt Busby and Bill Shankly. We won 8–0 and Matthews was sensational. His crosses to Tommy Lawton were inch perfect, and could not have been better placed had he used radar. It was in that game that Tommy first used the line, 'Stanley, can you please cross the ball with the lace facing away from me.' He was that good, I'm sure he could have done it. The best goal of the match was scored by Matthews himself. He waltzed around at least five Scottish defenders before taking the ball up to goalkeeper Joe Crozier and sending him the wrong way before passing the ball into the net. Even the Scottish players applauded that one."

Just three weeks after Denis's death in 1997, Sir Stanley Matthews was a guest of honour at the 50th Football Writers' annual dinner. He had been the first winner of their Footballer of the Year award in the 1947–48 season. Sir Stanley, looking nearer sixty than his eighty-two years, was still grieving over the passing of his old wartime team-mate.

Unique tricks
SIR STANLEY MATTHEWS: "It was fifty years ago that Denis was the talk of the nation because of his feats with the cricket bat. Had there been such an award then as the Cricketer of the Year, he would have won it hands down. Denis and I were together many times on and off the football pitch. He was a real charmer, and did not have an enemy in the world. I think it fair to say that the war cost him at least a dozen or so full England football caps. It was during the war years that he was at his absolute peak as a footballer with a lot of unique tricks in his larder. The only reason he and I were not closer friends is that he liked to imbibe on something of a grand scale, while I have never touched a drop in my life. But for all that, we were good mates. When Denis was holding court at the bar I would quietly slip away. I sometimes wonder what I missed because he always had his audience entertained, just as he did when batting or playing football. We served together in recent years on a sports committee, and even though he was having problems with his hips he still had that certain sparkle in his eyes. He was always a bit of a lad, you know. And everybody loved him for it."

Waving the flag
STAN CULLIS, one of the great England centre-halves and later master manager of all-conquering Wolves, was captain

for most of the wartime internationals in which Compo played: "There were times, to be honest, when I am not sure even Denis knew where he was going on his twisting, turning left-wing runs, but the end result was usually most productive for players like Tommy Lawton and Jimmy Hagan playing inside him. We all had a good laugh over a remarkable incident during a Victory international against Scotland at Hampden. Denis collected a pass from Jimmy Hagan, and set off on one of his dribbling adventures. As he centred the ball he lost his balance and collided with the corner flag, which broke at the base. A Scottish supporter came running on to the pitch, snatched the flag, waved it in Denis's face and then raced off with it back on to the terraces. It was one of the few times when an international match almost came to a halt because so many people were laughing."

Dangerous driving

BERNARD JOY: "My wartime memories of Denis are of a winger playing incredible football that was at one and the same time exhilarating and frustrating ... and of a driver who could frighten the life out of his passengers. Denis played his football like he played his cricket, with invention that could not be found in any coaching manual. He was absolutely brilliant in taking on and beating defenders, but it could be frustrating for his colleagues waiting for a pass that often came much too late. Our trainer Billy Milne used to lose sleep over the lovable rascal, who had a habit of turning up for a game at the last minute without boots or any sort of kit whatsoever. This was, of course, in the days when there was not a dressing-room staff to help out. I have known Denis go out on to the pitch in boots he had never seen before and win the match with blinding skill. He was not a prolific goalscorer, but when he did put the ball into the net it was usually something quite remarkable that would have everybody shaking their head in wonder. I quickly learned not to accept lifts from Denis. He seemed to have his mind on anything but driving, and to be driven through London by him during the days of the blackouts was not to be recommended. The man was a sporting genius, and would certainly have won official football caps to go with his cricket collection but for the war. I agreed with the popular assessment that Denis *played* cricket and *worked* at football. Cricket was, without question, his first love. Ted Drake, Joe Hulme, Les and Denis used to spend hours discussing cricket tactics and the merits of county sides, and the bets they were always striking with each other finished with the outbreak of war. The standing joke was that Arsenal would be able to beat any team in the League ... at cricket!"

Dazzling on the wing

WILF MANNION, the little maestro of Middlesbrough who was the Golden Boy of football when Denis was known as the Golden Boy of crickey: "Denis had terrific skill on the ball. He mostly used his right foot for standing on, but his left was worth two feet. I played in a wartime international against Scotland at Wembley in 1942 which was organised by the Prime Minister's wife, Mrs. Churchill, to raise funds to help Russia. Stanley Matthews was on the right wing and Denis on the left. They were both dazzling with their work down the touchline, and the Scottish full-backs were run ragged. Another time Denis and I played for the British Army against the French Army, and we ran up a cricket score. We used to rib Denis that he would do better if he wore cricket pads. He was good company off the pitch, and liked a glass or two. There is no doubt at all that he would have had several England caps to go with all his cricket honours but for the war during which he was at his peak as a footballer. By the time the war was over he had put on a few pounds and had lost a vital yard or two in pace. By then, of course, the great Tom Finney had come through as the number one outside-left. When you think of all that Denis achieved, particularly in cricket, the nice thing was that he was never big headed and was very easy-going and likable."

The County Cricket Championship was suspended until after the war and hastily arranged matches were casual affairs in which Denis was able to keep his eye in. The Oval became a prisoner-of-war camp, and Lord's was used for occasional games involving a select side called the Buccaneers, and British Empire XIs featuring mainly Australian and South African servicemen. Denis was an automatic choice for the Army XI, and scored eighty-seven for them against the RAF in seventy minutes just a week after an operation for the removal of varicose veins. It was young Alec Bedser who caught him out during a match in which they started a lifelong friendship. Denis also played regularly for London Counties in tandem with brother Les. While not the most nimble of men behind the stumps, the large-framed Les always used his enormous reach to good effect.

Bats, balls and bombs

LES COMPTON: "It was difficult to give full concentration to the cricket matches because they were often as not mad-dash one-day games between bombing raids. Denis was playing for the Army against the RAF at Lord's in 1940 when the sirens wailed to signal the first German aerial raid on London. They played on, not realising how serious it was until the sky became black with German bombers. Whether batting or bowling, Denis was in exceptional form during the limited wartime cricket. He averaged about ninety, and once took six wickets for eighty-odd in a ten-over spell against an all-star side that included the great Frank Woolley. Another performance that sticks in my mind was his 101 in just seventy minutes for a Plum Warner team against the Club Cricket Conference. Most of the time was spent getting the ball back from the boundary. It was London cricket's loss when Denis was suddenly posted overseas."

Compo's eventful life took another enormous turn in 1943 when he was posted to India. He marked his farewell appearance for Arsenal in the wartime Southern League with a hat-trick against Luton Town, and then the next day sailed to the subcontinent on the crowded troopship *Stratheden*, a sea journey that took four weeks. Just before embarking on his journey Denis was surprised to find himself promoted to sergeant-major. The usual mental picture conjured up of a sergeant-major is of a bellowing Windsor Davies-type making life hell for the bullied solders under his command. This image could not have been farther from Sergeant-Major D.C.S. Compton, British Army, India.

The beer run
DENIS COMPTON: "My job was to get British soldiers fit for the Burma campaign. Among the lads passing through were commandos on the way to top secret missions against the Japanese. These guys were tough enough to break me in two. I used to tell them, 'Look chaps, we've got to make it seem as if I'm giving you a hard time. I'm going to take you on a run and when you get back I want you to let the officers know what a b— I've been.' We would then run for a mile or so to a place where I had laid on some beer for the lads. Then we would run back looking exhausted. Those boys were going to have a hard enough time without me adding to it. I was also in charge of the weapons training of young Indian officers. One of them became the ruler of Pakistan."

When Denis told me this during my undercover research for his *This Is Your Life* tribute, I wondered if it was an exaggeration. Sue Green, a researcher with the show and later the programme's Producer, did some detective work and after a series of long-distance telephone calls reported, "It's true! General Zia remembers him and wants to film for the programme." Zia was considered a dictator with a suspect human-rights record, but Eamonn Andrews ruled that as his contribution would have no involvement with politics we should go ahead and film him. Eamonn liked nothing better than to have presidents and kings on his show. A film crew was sent to General Zia's headquarters, and he went on record with this tribute ...

Weapons training

GENERAL ZIA UR RAHMAN: "Denis, my good friend. You will probably not remember me but I was an officer cadet under you in the Cadet Infantry School at Mhow in 1944. I am glad to have this opportunity to thank you for all that you did to help mould me into a proper soldier. You were a very kind and understanding weapons training instructor, and my young colleagues and I were all in awe of your prowess at both cricket and football. I followed your career very closely and I congratulate you on having become one of the world's truly outstanding cricketers. I am very proud to say that I was trained by none other than Denis Compton. Thank you so very much, my friend."

Denis was overwhelmed by this warm tribute, and was able to tell me, "I told you so ... everybody thought I was making it up when I said that I had trained the future President of Pakistan." During his two years in India Denis played in regimental and Army representative football matches, several games of rugby as a flying left wing, and seventeen first-class cricket games. Eye-witnesses of his rugby performances said that he was, of course, unpredictable with his runs for the line. Compo was posted to a training school at Holkar and was invited to play for the state side in a Ranji Trophy match against Bombay. It remains in the *Wisden* bible of record books to this day as what was then the highest-scoring game of cricket ever played. There were 2,708 runs amassed, and Denis contributed 20 in the first innings and then 249 not out in the second. He thought it was an innings that was going to make him a small fortune.

Disappearing trick

DENIS COMPTON: "We went into the second innings needing the little matter of 863 runs to win the match! A wealthy local merchant came into the dressing-room before the start of the innings and announced, 'I will pay any batsman fifty rupees for every run that he scores over a hundred.' I have never paid so much attention to the number of runs that I was putting on the board. It was a sweltering hot day and I concentrated on trying to collect my runs in boundaries, and after I had passed the ton I began to calculate that I was earning 200 rupees every time I hit a four. I ran out of partners on 249 and we finished 374 runs off our target on a lifeless matting wicket. I looked out for my benefactor as I came off at the end, but he had done a disappearing trick. 'Oh, he left the ground when you got your two hundred up,' I was told. I reckon he owed me about five hundred pounds which I never saw. Oh well, that's life."

The underarm cut

REG SIMPSON, a Nottinghamshire master of the batting arts, was also serving with the British Army in India: "I played in the match in which Denis scored his first century on the subcontinent. We were selected for a Services XI against the Cricket Club of India, which was virtually their Test team. We all played in borrowed kit, and I remember that Denis had a shirt on that was so tight that he got a pair of scissors and cut under the armpits. It certainly worked for him because he scored 120-odd, but we got slaughtered by the Indians. Our attack was taken apart by Vijay Merchant, who rattled up a double century. The temperatures often soared above a hundred degrees, and all of us - including Denis - were as brown as berries. The wickets were bone hard and made for runs once you got your eye in. This gave you the confidence to go for your strokes, and the Indian spectators loved watching Denis going down the wicket after the spinners in his inimitable style."

As the Japanese were driven out of Burma, Compo was ordered to select a team of footballers from all the regiments in India to tour Burma and India for a series of matches aimed at bringing some entertainment to the "Forgotten Army". The side that Compo was able to choose all had pre-war League experience: Ted Ditchburn (Tottenham), John Milburn (Leeds), Cyril Trigg (Birmingham City), Bill Watson (Preston), Eric Hayward (Blackpool), Ivor Powell (QPR), George Stewart (Brentford), Harry Potts (Burnley), Stan Pearson (Manchester United), Syd Ottewell (Chesterfield) and Compo (Arsenal).

The entertainers

TED DITCHBURN, capped six times as England goalkeeper and last line of defence in the famous push-and-run Tottenham championship-winning team: "Denis was a very thoughtful captain, who gave more consideration to our refreshments after the match than to anything as mundane as tactics. He believed that we should all enjoy ourselves, and I can honestly say that was as happy a team as I ever played for. We took our lead from Compo, and played it all off the cuff. It must have been a success because we won all our matches, and the Tommies watching us always gave us a great reception. Mind you, after the war experiences they had been through against the Japs the football could only have come as a relief. The only orders Denis would give before each game were, 'Let's go out there and entertain them.'"

The Burma Road

DENIS COMPTON: "We travelled through India and Burma by Army lorry, and once on a drive through the jungle roads of Burma our driver was taken ill with malaria. I took over behind the wheel, and have never been so desperate to get a journey over and done with. There were still bands of armed Japanese on the loose, and I had the accelerator pressed down so hard it's a wonder my foot didn't go through the floor. We played local teams who usually turned out barefooted, but they could kick the ball every bit as hard as us in our boots. We also entertained the troops with concerts in which I used to do a turn singing 'Underneath the Arches' with British boxing champion Freddie Mills. Gracie Fields was top of the bill. After winning our final match in Mandalay we were ordered to travel on to Madras for an exhibition game against another touring services side that had been selected by Scottish international Tommy Walker. But I had to miss the game because of a cricket commitment."

Compo was the one Englishman selected to play for the East Zone of India against the Test-strength Australian Services team that stopped off in Calcutta after a successful tour of England. It brought him face to face with the man who over the next dozen years was to become his greatest foe and for the rest of his life his dearest friend: Keith Ross Miller. This meeting in India gave them cause for laughter ever after.

8: Golden Nugget

*Compo and I were like brothers. Of course, he
was a great cricketer. But, better than
that, he was a great companion.*
Keith Miller

FROM the day in 1945 that Flight Sergeant Keith Ross Miller walked away from his crash-landed war plane he lived every moment as if it was a bonus. The tall, debonair Australian from the appropriately named Sunshine district of Melbourne had a devil-may-care approach to life that made an instant impact on kindred spirit Denis Compton. They became deadly rivals on the cricket field, but inseparable buddies off it.

Quick introduction
DENIS COMPTON: "I remember the first time we came face to face was in a 1943 wartime charity match at Lord's between England and a Dominions services team. I was batting when the ball was tossed to this tall, leggy fellow with a mane of swept-back black hair that was longer than would have been allowed in our services. He had been playing to the crowd out on the boundary with spectacular fielding and throwing. I turned to Australian wicket-keeper Stan Sismey, and asked: 'What does this chap do, Stan?' He smiled as he replied, 'He's more of a batter than a bowler, but I think you might find him a bit on the quick side.' The new bowler, the fifth used by the Dominions, came in off a short run and unleashed a ball that was as quick as anything I had faced since Larwood in my first season. This was my introduction to Keith Miller."

91

"You must go ...!"

KEITH MILLER: "It was our second meeting that Denis and I always remember. The Australian Services team stopped off in Calcutta on the way back from a tour of England in 1945. We played what we thought would be an all-Indian East Zone side, but surprise, surprise, they had Sergeant-Major Compton guesting for them. We met up the night before the match at a reception given by the captain of the local football club. There had been a lot of ugly rioting in protest against British rule, and while Denis was batting the next day a mob of rioters invaded the pitch. The flag-carrying leader was none other than the chap who had been our party host. He approached Denis and said, 'You very good man, Mr. Compton, but you must go.' Denis and I were roaring with laughter as we walked off the pitch and left them to get on with their riot. From then on whenever Denis came out to bat against any team I was playing for I would say to him in a very exaggerated Indian accent, 'You very good man, Mr. Compton, but you must go.'"

Keith and I were colleagues on the *Daily Express* from the 1960s through to the seventies, and every summer he would visit the Fleet Street office to regale us with his treasure chest of stories. He was always at his best when Denis, then a *Sunday Express* columnist, joined the company, usually at Fleet Street watering holes El Vino's, Poppins or the Cheshire Cheese, or in the Albion on the corner of Ludgate Circus. We were always a noisy, happy, nicely lubricated crowd that usually included *Express* sports editor John Morgan, his effervescent deputy Norman Dixon, legendary columnist Desmond "The Man in the Brown Bowler" Hackett, king of the sports cartoonists Roy Ullyett and *Express* cricket correspondent Crawford White. We were also often joined by a young cricket statistician called Bill Frindall, later famous as the Bearded Wonder of the *Test Match Special* team. The following collection of stories is lovingly put together from those entertaining bar sessions and the reunion party that followed Compo's *This Is Your Life* tribute at which the Golden Nugget, as Denis called him, was a surprise fly-in guest from Oz.

One man too many
DENIS COMPTON: "Nugget was skippering New South Wales once and arrived for the game, not for the first time, with quite a hangover. As he was leading the team out on to the field and still struggling into his sweater having made a late arrival, one of the players said, "Scuse me, skip, but we appear to have twelve players.' Keith did not break his stride as he replied, 'Well one of you had better f— off ...'"

The winning ace
KEITH MILLER: "There was a match, I think it was at Old Trafford in 1948, when there were a lot of delays because of rain. Our regular card school of Compo, Godders [Godfrey Evans], Bill [Edrich], Ray [Lindwall] and myself got through a lot of poker hands in the pavilion. During one session a restart was announced when there was a big pot, something like thirty quid, on the table. I said, 'Right, chaps, first ace takes the pot.' I dealt the cards, came up with an ace for myself, scooped up the money and then walked out to the field with the rest of the guys gaping at me. Within minutes I was bowling flat out to Bill with bumpers that were whizzing around his head. Compo, down at my end, said, 'It's not enough that you take our pot, now you want to knock our blocks off as well!'"

The Queen's concern
DENIS COMPTON: "That was the match when I mishooked against a no-ball bouncer from Ray [Lindwall], and the ball whacked me on the forehead. Suddenly I was seeing more stars than an astronomer. I went off for stitches with four runs to my name, and managed to add another hundred

and forty-odd when I came back after five wickets had tumbled. Keith and Ray still showed no mercy and continued to hurl down their bouncers. We were good mates off the field, but that meant nothing when we were out in the middle and the Ashes were at stake. A few weeks later during the tea interval at the Oval Test we were introduced to the Queen, now the Queen Mother, and she said to me, 'Mr. Compton, how's your poor head? My husband and I saw the incident on television and were deeply concerned for you.'"

Betting signals

KEITH MILLER: "We had a lot of fun with our gambling. Neither Compo nor I could resist a bet, and we used to share information with each other. I used to get tips almost from the horse's mouth because jockeys like Scobie Breasley and Willie Snaith were very good buddies of mine. Denis and I worked out a series of hand signals so that we could let each other know how our horses had got on when either one was out in the middle. We were often like racecourse tic-tacs. Dear old Scobie once gave us a winner that romped in at ten-to-one and I was on the balcony at Lord's gesturing with two thumbs up to Compo, who was fielding at slip. A radio commentator caught sight of me and told his listeners, 'Keith Miller is giving enthusiastic encouragement to the batsmen from the players' balcony.' When we were both on the field with Denis batting, I would have the twelfth man signal how our horses had gone. If one of Compo's tips let us down, I used to let him know by bowling him a bouncer!"

Tea and sympathy

DENIS COMPTON: "Scobie Breasley was a great character, and Keith used to take him everywhere with him. He was a tiny man with heavily lined, craggy features. There was an embassy do before one of the Tests and Keith brought Scobie along. One of the snooty guests was almost disdainful of Scobie when he was introduced by Keith as a jockey ... until

Keith mischievously added, 'Of course, he's the Queen's jockey.' The change in the attitude and respect towards Scobie had Keith and I busting with suppressed laughter. Once, Keith and I were together for a charity match at the Vincent Square ground in London. It was on the day the Queen's horse, Pall Mall, was running in the Royal Hunt Cup at Ascot in the late 1950s. We'd had a few bob on it and were desperate to watch the race on television. There was not a set in the pavilion, and so we knocked on the door of one of the flats overlooking the ground and talked a lovely old lady into letting us watch her telly. She even served us with tea while we cheered on Pall Mall. Sadly, it didn't win and the old dear was most sympathetic."

On the nose

KEITH MILLER: "Our first big betting spree together was in Calcutta where Compo was treated like royalty. He was friendly with a Maharaja, who invited us to the races where he had a horse running. 'This horse of mine cannot be beaten,' he told us, so Compo and I piled in and put all our rupees on the nose. Not only was the horse beaten, but it trailed off last. From then on, Denis and I decided we would never again take the word of a Maharaja!"

One for the book

DENIS COMPTON: "My favourite betting story is of the day in 1947 when Keith introduced me to a bookmaker pal of his at a race meeting in Sydney. I wanted to put my tenner on a tip that I had been given, but the bookie refused to take the bet. 'That's got as much chance of winning as my old granny,' he said, putting my ten pounds into his satchel. 'I'll put your stake on such-and-such instead.' Sure enough, the horse selected by the bookie romped in at something like ten to one. Not only did he pay up, but as I was walking away he came racing after me. 'Sorry, Mr. Compton,' he said, handing me another ten pounds. 'I forgot to give you your stake money back.' It was the one and only time in my life when a bookmaker wanted to give me money rather than take it from me!"

A beamer, then beers
KEITH MILLER: "The nearest Compo and I came to falling out during a cricket match was in the fourth Test at Adelaide in 1947. He virtually played us on his own with a century in each innings, and drove us to frustration when shielding Godfrey Evans from the bowling. Godders went a record ninety-seven minutes without scoring, and Denis kept refusing to take singles despite our skipper Don Bradman spreading the field. 'This is not the way to play the game,' the Don said to Compo. He shrugged and replied, 'You set a proper field and I'll play proper cricket.' I got so worked up that I bowled a beamer at Denis that just missed his head and shot away for four byes. Compo was not amused, and I said, 'Sorry, mate, but you're beginning to bore me!' We had a few beers at the end of the day, and forgot all about it. In the next Test I grabbed a stump while running the winning runs and presented it to Compo as a mark of our friendship."

The fastest ball
DENIS COMPTON: "You never knew what Nugget would bowl next. He was one of the most unpredictable Test bowlers there has ever been. Sometimes he would come storming in off a long run and bowl a slow off-break, and then with the next ball turn and come at you off no more than six paces and let fly with a bumper. I recall him testing the Reverend David Sheppard's faith by bowling him with a googly, and on a Brisbane sticky once took seven for sixty with off-breaks. If he had been out on a hard-drinking night the previous evening then you could bet he would hit you with a barrage of bouncers to help get rid of his hangover. Another sign that he was about to let rip with a snorter was when he used to brush back that mop of hair of his with his

hand, in which he used to hold a tiny comb. Even if you punished his bowling he would still keep coming at you with fire and heart. I had scored 184 in the Trent Bridge Test in 1948 when he unleashed a short ball. I shaped to hook it but the ball came at me so quickly that I fell back into my stumps. Wicket-keeper Don Tallon told me later that it was the fastest ball he had ever seen Keith bowl."

On deaf ears

KEITH MILLER: "Don Tallon! What a character. We called him Deafy because he was hard of hearing. We were playing England at Trent Bridge in 1953 in half light and we were in a lot of bother against some magnificent swing bowling by Alec Bedser, who took fourteen wickets in the match. Don was sitting padded up ready to go in seventh wicket down, and our captain Lindsay Hassett said to him, 'When you get out there, Deafy, give the light a go.' Just a minute later a wicket fell and as Deafy prepared to walk out, the skipper shouted, 'Don't forget, give it a go as soon as you get out there.' Don joined Alan Davidson at the wicket and told him, 'Skipper says we've got to give it a go, Davo. Throw the bat at everything.' Don lashed out at every ball and was out off a skier after about five minutes. He returned to the dressing-room dragging his bat, and said to an open-mouthed Hassett, 'Sorry, Skip. I tried to give it a go, but I could hardly see the ball. The light's terrible out there.'"

The raised bat

DENIS COMPTON: "The incident that sums up Keith's approach to cricket came when he was playing against Essex at Southend in 1948. That was the famous match in which Australia scored a record 721 runs in just one day. Nugget went to the wicket with nearly 400 runs already on the board. Facing his first ball from Trevor Bailey, he raised his bat and allowed the ball to hit his stumps. He was too much of a caring sportsman to want any part of the massacre."

Most popular Pom

KEITH MILLER: "I remember attending a ceremony in Adelaide when Compo was presented with a watch by the South Australian Cricket Association for scoring two centuries in the same Test against us. All I can assume is that the watch had no hands because it didn't help him become a better timekeeper. The only thing he was always on time for was to place his bets. His cavalier approach to cricket really appealed to lovers of the game Down Under, and he was probably the most popular Pom in Australia. He was certainly popular with the fillies! In his youth Denis was just about the most handsome man in the entire world of sport, and he attracted young ladies like bees to a honeypot. The pair of us got up to a lot of things that young men do, but they remain secrets with Compo and me. Let's just say we thoroughly enjoyed ourselves."

Hair-raising adventures

DENIS COMPTON: "We have an unspoken pact that nobody will ever know all the things that Nugget and I got up to together. To be honest, I'm not sure either of us can remember everything. A lot of it was enjoyed in something of an alcoholic haze. Let's just say we had some pretty hair-raising adventures! But something I want to stress is that neither of us ever put our social life before our cricket. Mind you, there was the time when Keith was seen at Ascot in top hat and tails when he should have been out in the field. He had taken it for granted that the day's play would be called off because of heavy rain. Trouble was, it was not raining at the ground. When Nugget and I were out on the town or facing each other on the field, the world was just about a perfect place."

For the record, Denis and Keith played against each other in twenty-four Tests. Denis finished on the winning side only four times, with nine of the matches drawn. Keith played a part in Compo's dismissal eleven times, holding six catches, bowling him three times and getting him leg before in two Tests. Denis scored four centuries, Keith two. They were great rivals, even greater friends. It was a thrill to watch them, a pleasure to listen to them. We will not see their like again.

Back home, Compo had an even more famous alliance ...

9: The Terrible Twins

I will never understand why Denis was not given a knighthood. If the people had had their way, he would have been a lord.
Bill Edrich

BILL EDRICH came off his parents' Norfolk farm to harvest runs for Middlesex and England, and to forge a long-running partnership with Denis Compton. Their double act ran off the tongues of cricket followers as easily as Marks and Spencer, Laurel and Hardy, Fortnum and Mason and just about any famous pair you care to name. Compton and Edrich, particularly in the immediate post-war years, were inseparable and between them scored a total of more than 75,000 runs and played in 117 Test matches. They were nicknamed The Terrible Twins.

The *REAL* hero
DENIS COMPTON: "W.J. and I first met on the Lord's groundstaff when we were lads. It was the start of a friendship that lasted a lifetime. I have often been described as a hero, but W.J. was a *real* hero. While I was relatively swanning it down in India during the war he was a squadron leader flying dangerous daylight bomber missions over Germany. He was honoured with a Distinguished Flying Cross. It was Bill's wartime experiences that made him live his life with the throttle full out. He had five wives, and our standing joke was that I was best man at his third wedding and third man at his best wedding! Bill said he would not send out invitations to his fifth wedding because we all had season tickets. He had a fabulous sense of fun."

I tracked Bill down for his memories of Compo when Eamonn Andrews was first considering a *This Is Your Life* tribute to Denis. Eamonn, who treated each of his *TIYL* projects with MI5-style security, ordered me to swear Bill to total secrecy about the planned tribute. My brief was to get Bill reminiscing about his old partner and pal. Even in his late sixties, I discovered that Bill still had a twinkle in his eye and perhaps too strong a love for the hard stuff. He talked about Denis as if he was more brother than friend. Bill, or W.J. as Compo always called him, was of the strong opinion that the Establishment had let down his former running mate in a big way by not making him Sir Denis.

Political pawn
BILL EDRICH: "If the people who watch cricket had had their way it would have been Sir Denis long ago, or even Lord Compton! I have my own opinion why he has not been knighted. Denis and I made ourselves unpopular by speaking out in favour of keeping cricket links going with South Africa. We were not into politics. We just didn't like to see politicians interfering with sport. Both of us, particularly Denis, loved South Africa and we had some of the best moments of our lives out there. We were entitled to voice an opinion, but I'm sure that the controversy cost Denis a knighthood that he richly deserved. The only honour they have given him is a CBE, which he calls Caught and Bowled Edrich! But for his views on South Africa, I'm sure it would have been, 'Arise Sir Denis.' It is such a shame because he does not have a racist bone in his body. He just didn't see why cricket should be a pawn in a political game."

A closed subject
DENIS COMPTON: "The South African business is a closed subject as far as I'm concerned. I fell out with quite a few people over it, including John Arlott, David Sheppard and Michael Parkinson. But we buried our differences long ago.

I must admit it hurt me to be described as a racist, and a supporter of apartheid. The people making those accusations clearly did not see all the coaching I used to give to young black cricketers in the townships. I'm lucky to have been involved with sport all my life. I have never been, and have never wanted to be, a politician."

I was much more interested in talking sport than politics to both Denis and Bill. But that is not to gloss over the fact that both of the "Twins" felt they had been hard done by on the South African issue when they were pilloried for what were considered blinkered and naive views. I got Bill back on to the cricket track by asking him if he could recall the first match in which he and Compo played together.

Punctured egos
BILL EDRICH: "It was in 1935. We were selected as bowlers for the MCC against Beaumont College, a Jesuit school at Runnymede. Our skipper was a real toff of a character called Alec Waugh, brother of the writer Evelyn and himself a distinguished author. He put us in at ten and eleven. Denis joined me at the wicket as last man in and quickly raced to forty-five not out to my seventeen. We won by more than a hundred runs. In those days we used to go to matches by Green Line bus, usually on a single ticket. Denis would then use his charm to get us a lift back with one of our wealthier team-mates. We were a couple of scroungers in those days because money was really tight. It was a very strict regime at Lord's and we had to 'sir' everybody. For a Norfolk farm boy like me it was quite a jolt to the system to be treated with sheer arrogance by many MCC members, but Denis shrugged it all off and told me not to get so uptight. I used to get my own back on the snobs who looked down their noses at us groundstaff boys by bowling flat out at them when they requested practice nets. Denis used to bewilder them with spin, while I concentrated on speed. It was great

to puncture their egos by getting the ball to whistle around their ears."

A gashed hand
DENIS COMPTON: "Bill would have been too modest to tell you how he started at Lord's. The day before his trial he gashed his right hand in an accident with a horse on his father's farm. He had it bandaged, and did not tell anybody at Lord's what had happened in case they cancelled the trial. He had to go into the nets to face the bowling of coach George Fenner, who could spot any weakness in a batsman within seconds of seeing him shape up. Bill faced a variety of balls, and played them all with confidence despite feeling blood soaking his batting glove from the reopened wound. George realised something was wrong, and coaxed the story about the accident from Bill. I think it was there and then that George decided that Bill had the sort of guts needed to back up his skill as an all-round player. People always talk about Bill the batsman, but they tend to forget that he was also a fine fast bowler and one of the quickest around just after the war. He lived his life like he played his cricket, with the accelerator hard to the floor. Bill was a lovable extrovert."

Bill went too far with his merry making off the pitch during the 1950 Old Trafford Test against the West Indies. He was not out at the end of play on the Saturday and the next evening he took Godfrey Evans out to celebrate the Kent wicket-keeper's maiden Test century. It was the early hours of the morning when he returned to the team hotel in a less than sober state. He was so noisy that he woke up the man sleeping in the next room. It just happened to be Bob Wyatt, a selector and former England Test captain.

Banished to the sidelines
BILL EDRICH: "I continued my innings unaware that I had upset anybody. I had increased my score to seventy-odd

when Everton Weekes took a brilliant catch to dismiss me off the bowling of Sonny Ramadhin, who was making his Test debut along with Alf Valentine. We won the match by more than 200 runs and I was top scorer in that second innings. At the end of the match Bob Wyatt called me to one side and told me he was reporting me. He considered that my night out had impaired my batting. It was then suggested that I should voluntarily withdraw from the winter tour to Australia. I refused, and was punished by being pushed on to the Test match sidelines for three years. I have always said to Compo that he might easily have been my drinking partner that night but for that wretched knee of his that kept him out of the game. Everybody knows that I believed in having a good time off the pitch, but there is not a soul in this world who can ever point the finger and say that I ever gave less than 100 per cent when playing, whether for county or country. The same can be said for Denis. He liked to enjoy himself, but always stood up to be counted on the field of play right from our earliest days together."

Watch the birdie
DENIS COMPTON: "Those early days at Lord's were wonderful times despite the strict discipline. Bill and I were so lucky to have characters like Patsy Hendren and big Jim Smith prepared to take time out to give us tips and to keep us enraptured with their cricketing tales. Patsy was a powerfully built, cheerful cockney who was full of wisecracks and leg-pulling stunts. Fielding in the deep once with that exceptional cricketer/footballer Joe Hulme he realised that Joe had lost sight of a high ball going for the boundary. 'It's to your right, Joe!' he shouted, and then watched doubled up as Joe threw himself after a low-flying pigeon."

Silent assassin
BILL EDRICH: "I remember one match in which Jim Sims, who was always talking on the pitch, was suffering from

laryngitis. He coached us in the dressing-room on how to help with his appeals, and every time he thought he had a wicket he would wave his arms like a conductor and we would shout in unison, 'Owzat!' He took seven wickets that day and we dubbed him the Silent Assassin. When I first joined Middlesex Jim Smith used to be the life and soul of the dressing-room, and to this day I have not seen a bigger hitter of the ball. I once saw him hammer a delivery from Lancashire's Dick Pollard yards over the top of Father Time at Lord's. His favourite saying as he used to go out to bat was, 'I'm going to show the bowlers the name of the makers of my bat.' He was a fine bowler, of course, and he jokingly used to get hold of our head groundsman Harry White by the throat and say, 'When are you going to prepare a pitch for us bowlers instead of always with the batsmen in mind?'"

A team of Edriches

DENIS COMPTON: "W.J., of course, came from an incredible cricketing family. They used to field a complete team of Edriches in Norfolk, and Bill never lost his love for his native county. He went back to play for them after retiring from first-class cricket and skippered them well into his fifties. We shared the captaincy at Middlesex for a short spell, and then Bill took over on his own. I was never really cut out for the captaincy business. Let's be honest, I was never the best organised person on this planet! W.J. loved cricket and gave an awful lot to the game without getting too much in return. Remember that he played in the days when the money was quite pitiful. In fact Bill found himself better off by reverting to amateur status."

Never run out

BILL EDRICH: "I would like to make something clear about Denis. He was nowhere near as bad running between the wickets as all the stories suggest. In all the years that we played together he never once ran me out. Mind you, I have to admit there were some close calls. I would often hear a roar from the crowd and look back down the wicket to find Denis scampering home with his bat left stranded in the middle of the pitch. It was our skipper Walter Robins who first said that when Denis called for a run it was just the basis for negotiations. All you had to do was keep alert when Denis was on strike and you could get your run in provided you gave a proper call. Sometimes we used to get in a tangle because we would be laughing so much. Cricket was fun then, you know."

Shipboard fun and games
DENIS COMPTON: "Some of the best fun we had was on board ships when going off on tours. It was all so much more leisurely in those days when we used to take weeks getting to our destination. We used to do our training on deck, and then in the evenings get plenty more exercise by joining in the dances. I recall that when sailing on the *Stirling Castle* from Southampton for the 1946-7 Ashes tour Bill got very drunk one night and I had to try to get him to his cabin without skipper Wally Hammond seeing that he had over-indulged. Mind you, Wally could do his share of elbow bending but, as captain, he could claim it was all part of his social duty. I was holding W.J. up against his cabin door when an elderly couple pushed past us on their way to their cabin. Goodness knows what they thought we were up to, but I heard the wife say, 'Quite disgraceful. Surely they could wait until they get into their cabin!'"

Wandering eye
BILL EDRICH: "I was between marriages on one of the trips out to Australia and was allowed a wandering eye. Denis told me that there was a certain lady who had expressed a keen interest in me. When I moved in on her and asked her for a dance I found that, one, she could not speak a word of English, and, two, her husband was at least nine feet tall.

That was a typical piece of Compo winding-up. He was a lovable rascal with what could be an impish sense of humour."

Cold-shower treatment

DENIS COMPTON: "Bill always liked a drink or three, particularly if ever he met up with an old RAF chum. He bumped into one on the eve of the second Test in Sydney in 1947. W.J. and I were sharing a room and I was surprised to find when I woke up on the morning of the first day's play that Bill's bed had not been slept in. I rumpled his bedclothes to make it look as if he had spent the night there because I knew skipper Wally Hammond had a habit of dropping in unannounced. Sure enough, Wally arrived a few minutes later to talk about the game. 'Where's Bill?' he asked. 'Oh, uh, didn't you see him on your way here?' I said, trying desperately to think of a cover story. 'He's gone for an early morning jog. It's part of his match-day fitness programme.' Minutes after Wally had left the room Bill arrived looking like death warmed up. He was still wearing his dinner jacket, and he had an almighty hangover. 'I've drunk the night away with an old pilot chum,' he said. While he undressed I ran a cold shower, and pushed him under it. We were just in time for the team coach, and as luck would have it Bill had to go in to bat after we had lost an early wicket. I crossed my fingers as he faced his first ball, which I'm sure he could not have seen through his still bloodshot eyes. He showed just what character he had by top scoring in our innings with seventy-one and then knocking up a century in the second innings. Bill and I were always getting each other out of scrapes, but this one could have cost him his Test place if Wally had found out. What a character W.J. was. Do you know that in the fifty-odd years that we knew each other we never once had a cross word. We exasperated each other a lot of times, but never to the point where we fell out. He was as great partner and a great pal. I miss him terribly."

Bombing mission

BILL EDRICH: "Denis and I were never envious of each other. The more runs he scored the happier I was, and Denis was always encouraging me to keep up with him. Mind you, there was a time when he stopped me from scoring. I was playing for the RAF against the Army at Lord's. It was the day after it had been announced in the press that I had been awarded the DFC after a successful bombing mission to Cologne. The crowd gave me a standing ovation all the way to the wicket. That's a lovely memory. I had just got off the mark and then unleashed a towering shot towards the pavilion. A certain Army sergeant sprinted thirty yards to make a blinding catch. It was, of course, D.C.S. 'Sorry W.J.' he said to me later as we broke open the bubbly in celebration of my award. 'It's all right,' I told him. 'That's cricket.'"

Bravest of the brave

DENIS COMPTON: "I cannot believe that a braver man than W.J. walked on to a cricket field. He showed his courage time and again during his wartime bombing missions when he continually cheated death. Then there was the time when he had his cheekbone shattered by a rising ball from a then unknown Northants bowler called Frank Tyson. It was late in the afternoon and I was supposed to have been next man in. But as acting skipper I had no doubt that Bill would see us through to the close, and so I climbed into the bath. Bill and I were going out to dinner that evening. Suddenly, just as I stretched back in the water, there was a yell from the dressing-room. 'Quick, Skip,' came the shout, 'Bill's in trouble.' By the time I had dressed, Bill was being carted off to hospital with his cheek swollen like a balloon. He reported back to the ground the next morning looking in a grotesque state, with his jaw in a sling and his face black and blue and swollen. Making it almost comic was the fact that he had his pipe jutting out of the side of his mouth. Anybody else but Bill would have accepted that cricket was out of the question for at least a month. But he insisted he was going to continue his innings that morning. None of us, not even the umpires, could talk him out of it. 'Look,' he said, 'I've seen comrades blown out of the sky, and others who have carried on flying with terrible wounds. I'm not going to let the little matter of a fractured cheekbone stop me batting.' He went out and again faced Tyson, who quite rightly did not show him any mercy. Bill stood up to him, and collected another twenty or so runs before finally being caught. A little over a week later, with the side of his face now depressed where the ball had hit him, he faced Tyson again in the return match and scored a century."

A drop of the Irish

BILL EDRICH: "There was the famous occasion when Denis and I were introduced to Irish coffee for the first time. We had been invited to Dublin to open a new cricket ground, and it was agreed that during a formal dinner that evening Denis and I would make speeches about Anglo-Irish cricket relationships. We both enjoyed some typical Irish hospitality before the dinner, and decided we had better cut down on the drinking or our speeches would be unintelligible. Our host suggested that we stick to Irish coffee. 'It's mostly cream,' he said. What he happily forgot to mention was the double Irish whiskey in each cup. After three cups each Denis and I were flying higher than one of my old Blenheim bombers. Denis was first up, and he somehow managed to deliver a speech that just about made sense despite the slurring. Then it was my turn. I struggled to my feet and said, 'Gentlemen ...' That was all I could remember of my speech, and so I launched into the song, 'When Irish Eyes Are Smiling.' Denis started to join in, and then everybody in the audience took it up. It was the best reception I ever got for one of my speeches. Another time Denis and I were both making speeches at a dinner for Middlesex members during our run spree of 1947. I was halfway through my turn when

Denis pushed a note in front of me that read, 'Your flies are undone.' Of course they weren't, but you try stopping yourself looking down. All right, it was juvenile, but it was fun. And Denis and I had plenty of that when we were together."

A couple of cards
DENIS COMPTON: "Bill and I loved a game of cards, and there always had to be money in it to give it an edge. One day we were into a game of brag in a school that included several of the younger Middlesex players. Our captain Gubby Allen happened to walk into the room, and saw a pile of money in the middle of the table amounting to a pot of nearly one hundred pounds. Gubby summoned Bill and me, and said out of the hearing of the lads: 'It's not good for team spirit you taking all that money off those young boys.' Bill opened his arms and said, 'But, Skip, all that money in the middle is Denis's and mine. We're bidding against each other.'"

I was under orders from Eamonn Andrews to get a non-cricketing story with which to bring Bill Edrich on to the *This Is Your Life* set. Eamonn was keen that the programme should not become a sports documentary. He wanted a show that would reveal Compton the man. It was Bill who came up with an idea that appealed to Eamonn. He wanted to come on carrying a shove-halfpenny board!

The shove-halfpenny kings
BILL EDRICH: "Denis and I were terrors on the shove-halfpenny board. We used to play for hours in the pavilion during any rain delay or when the opposition were fielding. In fact we got so good that we used to take on challenges from pub teams, and always beat them. We had the best–polished board in the country, and it was as well looked after as any of our cricket equipment. Jim Sims was about to go

The young Compo catches Lindsay Hassett off the bowling of Hedley Verity during his first Test against Australia at Trent Bridge in 1938. Denis marked his debut against the Aussies with a century. At 20 years 19 days, he was England's youngest century-maker. *Popperfoto*

What no wicket-keeper? This was a specially posed photograph of Compo in the autumn of 1950 before he joined the MCC tour party for the trip to Australia during which he was vice-captain to Freddie Brown. Compo admitted that it was the most miserable tour of his career. He could hardly put bat to ball, and averaged just 7.57 in the Test series with a highest score of 23. To add to his misery, Compo missed out on a trip to Hollywood. *PA News*

Compo 1948. His greatest season behind him, this is a portrait of Denis in the summer dominated by Don Bradman's all-conquering Australians, who went through their tour undefeated. Compo managed to score two memorable centuries against an attack led by Lindwall and Miller. He amassed 184 runs in the first Test at Trent Bridge, and an undefeated 145 in the third Test at Old Trafford after mishooking a bouncer from Lindwall into his forehead and having to leave the pitch for stitches. *PA News*

Compo 1984. This is Compo 40 years on from the 1948 portrait above. The dark Brylcreemed hair is now white and the good looks are carrying the lines of a life well lived. He was 66 when this photograph was taken, a recent new father and content with the world. This was the year that Eamonn Andrews first planned to hit him with the big Red Book, but his *This Is Your Life* tribute had to wait two years following the passing of, first, his brother Leslie and then his old partner Bill Edrich. *PA News*

Rival captains Denis Compton (left) and Bill Edrich toss before the start of a match in 1949. Can you guess the ground on which the game is about to be played? Clue: Denis was at home there on the wing. It's Highbury Stadium, where Arsenal staged a cricket match as part of Compo's benefit year, with Middlesex playing Arsenal. *Popperfoto*

Compo in Madame Tussaud's? No. This was Denis modelling 'a double-breasted lounge suit in grey diagonal wolsted' at the 1952 Wool Secretariat Exhibition at the Royal Festival Hall. It was one of the many modelling, media and personal appearances that made him one of the top-earning sportsmen of the 1940s and 1950s. *PA News*

Compo the Footballer, above, duels with Burnley defender Arthur Woodruffe during a 1948 First Division match. Denis played just 54 first-team League games for Arsenal, losing the peak years of his career to the war during which he played in 14 unofficial internationals for England. *PA News*

Compo training for League football with Arsenal at Highbury in April 1949 (left), after returning from the South African tour during which he scored his world record 300 runs in 181 minutes. Compo had put on more than a stone and the extra weight was to cost him a vital yard in pace during the following football season that climaxed with him retiring after collecting an FA Cup medal against Liverpool at Wembley. *PA News*

King George VI is introduced to the Arsenal players by skipper Joe Mercer before the kick-off to the 1950 FA Cup Final at Wembley. Compo is alongside Arsenal right winger Freddie Cox. It was to be the last match but one for Denis before knee problems forced his early retirement. *Popperfoto*

Their Cup runneth over. This was the proudest day in the footballing careers of the Compton brothers when they shared Arsenal's FA Cup triumph against Liverpool at Wembley in 1950. In the same year, Leslie became the oldest England footballer to win a first England cap at the age of 38. *Popperfoto*

Two remarkable photographs taken 36 years apart. That's Compo above with his boyhood hero, Sir Jack Hobbs, on The Master's 70th birthday. They were pictured together in the BBC Radio Sports Report studio on December 16 1952 when they were interviewed by Eamonn Andrews. And Compo is himself 70 not out (right), with his old rival and closest pal, Keith Miller, keeping wicket. This picture was taken at Lord's on May 23 1988. *PA News*

Compo celebrates his 75th birthday at his second home, Lord's, on May 23 1993. In his prime, he was accustomed to raising his bat to acknowledge the cheers. He gets just as big a response with a glass of his favourite bubbly. *PA News*

The time: 1953. The place: The Oval ... and one of the most memorable matches of Compo's career. His four off the bowling of Arthur Morris was the shot that clinched the Ashes victory for England against Australia. Fittingly, his long-running partner Bill Edrich was at the other end. *Popperfoto*

J.J. (John) Warr, Compo's close friend and former Middlesex team-mate, had the Westminster Abbey congregation rocking with laughter with his memories of The Great Entertainer. 'If he did study a coaching manual,' he said, 'he must have been holding it upside down.' *PA News*

Westminster Abbey was packed as a congregation of 2,000 gathered to say a fond farewell to Compo at a Thanksgiving Service for his Life on July 1 1997. Former Prime Minister John Major was among them, and is seen here paying his respects to Denis's widow, Christine, who attended the service with daughters Charlotte and Victoria. *PA News*

in to bat once when he said in a sudden panic, 'Where is it ... has somebody stolen it ...?' I thought he was referring to his bat, and pointed to it. 'Not my bat,' he said. 'The board. It was here in my bag.' I nodded to the far side of the dressing-room where Jack Young and Denis were locked in a battle of shove-halfpenny. Panic over. It was a relieved Jim Sims who went out to bat."

Sadly, W.J. died before the *This Is Your Life* tribute to Denis. He passed away on the first day of the 1986 cricket season at the age of seventy. It was St George's Day, 23 April. Extraordinarily, Denis died on exactly the same day eleven years later.

Bill left behind as a monument to his cricketing ability a collection of 35,965 runs at an average of 42 despite losing his peak years to the war during which, as Denis said, he was a *real* hero. He scored 86 centuries, and took 479 wickets, first as a whippy-action fast bowler and then with off-spin. In 39 Test matches he scored 2,440 runs, including 6 centuries, and took 41 wickets. He was also a useful prewar winger with Tottenham. W.J. returned home to his beloved Norfolk for his final shots and skippered his county in minor cricket into his late fifties.

It is somehow comforting to know that on the day that he died following a fall down a flight of stairs at his home, Bill had partied well and drunk more than his share at a St George's Day luncheon that Denis missed because he was unwell. W.J. Edrich DFC always played his cricket with boyish enthusiasm and lived life to the full. The world was a poorer place without him.

Compton and Edrich, The Terrible Twins, have a permanent place in the record books - and at the Lord's ground where they shared so many of their partnerships. In the summer of 1991, Compo declared open the Compton and Edrich stands that have been erected side by side at the Nursery End of their favourite hunting ground. "I know that Bill will be Up

There with a glass of bubbly in hand sharing in this wonderful moment," Denis said. "But like me, he will be asking the question, "How on earth could they erect two stands bearing our names without a bar between them?'" They enjoyed many champagne moments, both on and off the field.

The exploits of Compton and Edrich, the Middlesex Twins, will never be forgotten - particularly those of the golden summer of 1947 ...

10: The Summer of '47

*I could not be more delighted that it is
Denis who has taken my record.
He has been a joy to behold. -*
Jack Hobbs

THE blazing summer of 1947 came in on the icy coat tails of
one of the coldest winters on record. The haunting horrors
of war were still a nightmare in the memory, and much of
the damage caused by Hitler's bombs had yet to be cleared.
It was the Age of Austerity, with appetites ruled by ration
books and there were petrol coupon restrictions on
motorcars. On to this bleak stage strode the Middlesex Twins,
lighting the darkness with the sunshine of their batting. Never
in the field of cricket have so many runs been plundered by
so few in just one season.

A cold start
DENIS COMPTON: "It's strange to think back on that season
and realise that I struggled to get runs in the first few weeks.
The summer got off to a cold and miserable start, and so
did I, managing only two hundred-odd runs in my first eight
innings. If anybody had told me then that by the end of the
season I would have nearly four thousand runs to my name
they would have been dismissed as being quite dotty. Then
the sun came out, and I moved up a gear with a quickish 150
for Middlesex against the South African tourists at Lord's at
the end of May. From then on I just could not stop scoring
runs, and most of the time good old W.J. was at the other

end also making the scorer work overtime. We used to challenge each other by saying, 'First one out buys the first round.' We got very thirsty that summer with all the running that we did."

Cricket in the corridor

BILL EDRICH: "It was a joy and a privilege to share the wicket with Denis. Nobody, and I mean nobody, has seen batting like it, and I had the best view of all of most of the runs that flowed from his bat in that golden summer. We had a lot of fun on the way to scoring more than seven thousand runs between us. I remember particularly an extremely jolly Saturday night in Leicester at the end of the first day's play. Our skipper Walter Robins missed the match and in my role as acting captain I decided the lads needed to unwind a little. We had a bit of a party that ended in the early hours of Sunday morning with an impromptu game of cricket in the corridor of Leicester's Grand Hotel. I provided the ball by climbing out of my bedroom window and along a ledge to Denis's room. Don't ask me why I did not go the orthodox way through the doors. Logic disappears when you've had a good drink. Anyway, I took a brass knob from Compo's bed and we used that as the ball. I tossed it to the Hon. Luke White, later the fifth Lord Annaly – and he opened the bowling, while I batted with his umbrella. Yes, we really enjoyed ourselves that summer. Incidentally, we won the match against Leicester when Denis and I knocked off the sixty-six runs needed in the last twenty-five minutes with four minutes to spare. Oh yes, it was great fun."

The sun seemed to shine all day every day, and it rained runs from the bats of Compton and Edrich. There is a full statistical breakdown at the back of this book, but just to summarise: in the summer of 1947 Denis scored 3,816 runs off his own bat, including an all-time record eighteen centuries, beating by two the previous record set by Jack

Hobbs. Bill contributed 3,539 runs, including twelve centuries. Both of them overtook Tom Hayward's record aggregate for a season. The Terrible Twins were just unstoppable. They put on 370 for England against South Africa at Lord's and 228 in the Old Trafford Test, and they shared four double-century stands for Middlesex.

The nervous nineties
DENIS COMPTON: "There was only one time when I almost froze. It was in the second innings against Lancashire at Lord's. I went to the wicket knowing that I needed just one more century to equal the record of sixteen centuries set by the great Jack Hobbs. You have to remember that to me Sir Jack was a god, and to think I was close to emulating my boyhood hero suddenly struck home when I reached ninety. As you know, I was never one for keeping a check on records. I was happy to let other people do the counting, but the papers were so full of the fact that I was close to the Hobbs record that I suddenly became nervous for the only time that summer. It took me half an hour to knock off the ten runs to take me to the ton, and the roar from the twenty thousand crowd showed that they were as relieved as I was when the three figures went up on the scoreboard. It was an unforgettable moment in my life. Sir Jack was one of the first to send me a telegram of congratulations when I overtook his record a few days later."

A tribute from Sir Jack
SIR JACK HOBBS: "I could not be more delighted that it is Denis who has taken my record. I have followed his career closely from day one, and enjoy the way that he plays the game. He is a charming young man with a deep love for cricket and he conveys this spirit at the wicket. Each time we meet he always makes a point of telling me that I was an inspiration to him when he was a schoolboy. I am very proud to think that I have helped in any way to shape him into

such an outstanding batsman. His batting this season has been a joy to behold."

Innovation at the wicket
ARCHIE FOWLER, Compo's old coach, was moved to make a statement near the close of the record-breaking season as youngsters around the country flourished their bats and tried to play the Compton way: "A lot of tosh has been written this summer about Denis not even bothering to have any net practice. I have helped him loosen up by bowling to him in the nets at Lord's for fifteen minutes before most home matches. He concentrates on playing it straight just to get his eye in, then he goes out and plays the most outrageous late cuts and sweep shots that are his own innovations. It is marvellous to watch, but you cannot say to a young lad, 'that's the way to play.' It all comes instinctively to Denis. It is not possible to coach anybody to bat the way that he does. He is a one-off. What I would say to any youngster trying to copy him is that they must first of all get their technique right. Denis has a solid knowledge of knowing how to play correctly. Everything else has been built on this foundation."

Straightest of sixes
DOUG INSOLE, later to become Essex captain and chairman of the TCCB, was just starting out on his first-class career in 1947: "I was in awe of Denis. He lit up that season like a beacon. I have never seen a more entertaining or more innovative batsman. His skipper Walter Robins once teased him during the tea interval of a match against Essex at Lord's that he could play shots all round the wicket but not the classic straight drive. Denis said to our bowler Ray Smith as he walked out with Robins to resume his innings, 'Your third ball is going to go over your head, so watch out.' It was not said in a cocky or arrogant way because that was not his style. It was just a statement of fact. Sure enough Denis hit Ray's third delivery high over his head for a very straight

and glorious six. Denis then nodded down the wicket to his skipper, who waved his bat in acknowledgement."

A single bus ticket
TOM GODDARD, jovial Gloucestershire off-break bowler, enjoyed his jousts with Compo, even when on the receiving end in that summer of 1947: "Denis gave me some fearful hammer on his way to two hundred and plenty for Middlesex against the Rest at the Oval. He lost his footing coming down the wicket to one of my flighted balls, and as he lay flat out he steered the ball to the boundary. We had a good laugh, and I told him that there would come a time when there would be no return ticket. The following season I managed to beat him with spin, and he was stumped four yards out of his ground. As he walked past me on the way to the pavilion I handed him a single bus ticket that I had been carrying in my pocket in the hope that I could trap the rascal. It was a pleasure to play against him even when he was knocking you all over the place. It was always fun and never boring when Denis was at the wicket."

The South African tourists were the main victims of the Compton run bombardment. On 4 September 1947 he plundered his sixth century of the summer off them to break the Hobbs record. Skipper Walter Robins and Bill Edrich came to the wicket carrying a tray on which was a bottle of milk and a glass. Denis toasted his record, with a champagne celebration coming later. He virtually gave away his wicket next ball, going down the track in characteristic style to South African slow left arm spinner Tufty Mann. He missed the ball and was stumped.

The flashing bat
ALAN MEVILLE, captain of the South Africans, tried not to look shell shocked as he paid tribute to Compo at the end of the tour in which Denis scored an aggregate 1,187 runs

against them including six centuries: "Denis has ensured that none of us who took part in this tour will ever forget this summer. His batting, not only against us but against most of the English County sides, has been of a calibre rarely seen before, and on behalf of my South African colleagues I warmly congratulate him on his record performances. You may think we are sick and tired of the sight of Denis and his flashing bat, but he has scored with such style and good spirit that it has been almost enjoyable watching him accumulate his runs against us. Take away his contribution, and I think it fair to say that our two teams were fairly evenly matched."

Breaking the record

O.C. [OSSIE] DAWSON, South African all-rounder, reminiscing on the 1947 tour with tongue firmly in cheek: "I wouldn't want it thought that Compo was impossible to get out that year, after all I managed to dismiss him twice. The first time he had made a little matter of 115 runs and the second 113. Yes, you could say that he was something of a nuisance. My lasting impression of him is of a marvellous person. He always came into our changing-room to have a friendly chat, never to gloat. Denis was a regular and very welcome visitor to South Africa and was always refreshing company. There was one moment in 1947 when I might have got the better of him. It was our last match, against the South of England at Hastings. I made my only hundred of the tour, 166, and was pretty pleased when the last fifty came in forty-five minutes. When the South batted, Denis only got 101. He gave his wicket away, dancing down the crease to Tufty Mann. He did so because it was the innings which brought him his seventeeth hundred of the summer, breaking Jack Hobbs's record. Play was held up for five minutes while he was congratulated, and we South Africans were proud to be there on the field playing a supporting role. My own contribution was somewhat overshadowed."

Stumped Evans, bowled Compton

GODFREY EVANS: "Everybody remembers the summer of 1947 for Compo's batting, but I also recall it for his bowling! My Kent colleague Doug Wright, the wizard of leg spin, returned his best figures for England in the second Test against South Africa at Lord's. He took ten wickets in the match, and for what was one of the rare occasions in any match in which we played together I did not claim a victim off his bowling. Yet I claimed two stumpings off the bowling of Compo, who took four wickets with those unpredictable left-arm spinners of his. I think that gave Denis almost as much pleasure as all the runs he scored. In that same Test he shared a record third-wicket partnership of 370 with his old mate Bill Edrich. No prizes for guessing who would have got the Man of the Match award had that been around in those days. Denis would have had a sideboardful of awards in 1947."

It was against Doug Wright and his Kent colleagues that Compo played what many [including Denis] considered one of the greatest innings of his life. Wright had wrecked Middlesex in the first innings with seven wickets for ninety-two runs. Middlesex went into the final day at 135 for four and needing a mountain of 397 runs to win. Compo smashed, swept, cut, sliced and steered the ball to all parts of the Lord's ground until Kent were reduced to putting every player apart from the bowler and wicket-keeper, Godfrey Evans, in run-saving positions on the boundaries. Compo rattled off 168 runs, including a share of 161 runs in ninety minutes in an astonishing stand with George Mann. Just as it looked as if he was going to win the match off his own bat Denis tried once too often to lift Wright to the boundary and was caught. His greatest innings did not create a victory. The last five wickets fell for twenty-five runs, and Kent became one of the few teams to beat Middlesex in a season when they romped away with the County Championship.

Simply magnificent

DOUG WRIGHT, interviewed immediately after the Kent victory: "I claimed Denis's wicket twice in this match, but I confess that during that second innings I was at a loss how to bowl to him. No matter how I flighted the ball and what line and length I took or how much spin I imparted he dispatched me with what seemed ease. It was almost as if he knew what I was going to bowl before I did, and he was advancing down the wicket the second I released the ball. At one stage, Godfrey Evans joked to Denis, 'Was it something we said?' I have never seen an innings to match it. It was quite breathtaking, and I salute Denis for a knock that was simply magnificent. While not helping my averages, he gave everybody great entertainment."

For any cricket follower of a certain age, there was always one writer's opinion that was respected above all others. Sir Jack Hobbs was The Master of batting, Neville Cardus The Master of writing. Cardus, who graced the pages of the Manchester *Guardian* with his beautifully composed cricket reports, was witness to many of the Compton centuries, and he captured better than anybody what it was like to be there on the sidelines watching a genius at work in that long hot summer of '47 ... One genius reporting on another ...

This happy cricketer

NEVILLE CARDUS: "Genius – even genius – needs to choose the right moment. Denis Compton came to the high summer of his renown in a period when we all badly wanted the like of him on our fields, for the purpose of rejuvenation. His cricket, in 1947, gave a nationwide pleasure which was somehow symbolical. In a world tired, disillusioned and threadbare, heavy with age and deprivation, this happy cricketer spread his favours everywhere, and thousands of us, young and old, ran his runs with him. Here at any rate was something unrationed. There were no coupons in an innings by Denis Compton. He was contagious; he liberated impulses checked for long amongst all sorts and conditions of English folk – women as well as men, girls as well as boys. He embraced a new public in search of entertainment and release, a public which knows nothing of the old divisions that restricted sport to 'men's games.' Denis hath his fans not less dewy eyed than those of Hollywood."

Attacking cricket

DENIS COMPTON: "A lot of flattering things were said about my batting in 1947, but I don't think enough credit was given to W.J. and the rest of the Middlesex team. Our skipper Walter Robins was the man who set the tone with his demand for attacking cricket. He would set us targets of 400 runs before tea. It sounds crazy now, but it is a fact ... and we usually managed to get them. Our openers Jack Robertson and Syd Brown would lay the foundation, and the shine would have been knocked off the ball by the time Bill and I got to the wicket. We would motivate each other, and once we had got our eye in have competitions to see who could score the quickest. During the intervals, Walter would tell us what declaration target he had in mind and that would make us put our foot even harder on the accelerator."

Nothing to match it

BILL EDRICH: "Both Denis and I get annoyed when we read modern articles by people who were not there sneering at the records that we set. They say that the bowling we faced was of a poor standard. Tell that to the likes of Alec Bedser, Doug Wright, Trevor Bailey, Roy Tattersall, Cliff Gladwin, Tom Goddard and Jim Laker, who were just some of the bowlers around at the time. I got a close-up view of D.C.S. in full flow, and I am telling you that he was just untouchable. One record that did not find its way into *Wisden* is that during the summer of 1947 the Middlesex team must have set some sort of record for drinking celebratory champagne. Denis and I had a bottle of bubbly after most of our centuries, and the entire team joined in when we won the championship – even lovely Jack Robertson, who was usually a strictly straight orange man. Jack Young, who was not only a fine spin bowler but the Middlesex poet, used to set our taste buds working by quoting Keats to us while we were out in the field:

> 'Oh, for a draught of vintage, that hath been
> Cool'd a long age in the deep delved earth.'

By the time we came off the field we were in the mood to drink the nearest bar dry, and we often did. I don't want this to sound as if we were alcoholics. It was just such a long hot summer and we did an awful lot of running. A good drink at the end of a hard day's play was our reward. Denis deserved every drop."

The fickle finger of fate was waiting to give Compo a nasty prod during a crescendo of a climax to what his more scholarly colleagues were calling his *annus mirabilis.* Playing for Middlesex against The Rest at the Oval in August in one of his last games of that record-shattering 1947 season he badly twisted his already bandaged right knee when dancing down the wicket to hit Tom Goddard to the boundary on his way to a season's highest score of 246 runs. During the next eight years the Compton Knee was to become almost as big a topic as his run making.

11: The Compton Knee

Denis was not only a quite exceptional batsman,
but also a very courageous one.
Peter May

DENIS COMPTON's right kneecap is on show at the Lord's museum. It sits in a tin container in the same history-drenched room as the Ashes in their famed brown wooden urn. Bill Tucker donated the kneecap to Lord's after he and fellow orthopaedic surgeon Osmond Clarke had carried out a series of operations on the knee that became a subject of national debate. There were regular bulletins on the 'Compton Knee' as former rugby international Tucker and Clarke tried first to prolong and then save Compo's career. We need to go back to the early days of his football career for the start of the problem.

One thing is certain: Denis first damaged the knee against Charlton Athletic in 1938 when colliding with the goalkeeper. The question is: which goalkeeper? I sat between Denis and former Charlton goalkeeper Sam Bartram in the press box at The Valley one afternoon in the 1960s. Denis was reporting for the *Sunday Express* and Sam for *The People*. Sam pointed to the spot where he said that he had sent Denis sprawling when making a save at his feet. "That," said Denis, "was the start of my knee trouble."

Yet in various interviews, including one with his skilled biographer Tim Heald [*Pavilion Books* 1994], he names Charlton reserve goalkeeper Sid Hobbins as the man responsible for first damaging his knee, and Sid in fact wrote

123

a post-war letter to Denis apologising for all the agony he had caused him. Hobbins played only two first-team games for Charlton compared with more than five hundred by Bartram.

I delved into old newspaper files for the answer, and found that Denis was left hobbling after colliding with Bartram while playing for the Arsenal first team. But the serious injury came in a reserve match when he was carried off after falling over the diving Sid Hobbins. He was later admitted to hospital for a cartilage operation.

Twinges of pain
DENIS COMPTON: "The main reason I retired from football was because of the continual twinges of pain that I got from the knee. I privately discussed it with Arsenal manager Tom Whittaker, an outstanding physiotherapist who knew everything there was to know about joints. He gave me a series of manipulative exercises to follow and talked me out of hanging up my boots at least a year before the 1950 FA Cup Final. Even in that wonderful summer of 1947 I was often in agony. In later years I was on and off the operating table so often that I was on first-name terms with everybody in the theatre. It got to the stage in 1955 when I just could not bend the knee, and the decision was taken that the kneecap had to come off. I soldiered on, but to be honest I was not 100 per cent fit for the last five or so years of my cricketing career. At times I was literally batting on just one good leg."

Football to blame
BILL EDRICH: "Denis never used to moan or groan about his knee, although those of us close to him knew that he was having a hellish time with it. It was the wear and tear of all those years sprinting up and down the left wing, twisting and turning and riding tackles. Football was more to blame than cricket. It was odd that it was the right knee that gave

him all the trouble because he used to do nearly all his tricky dribbling with his left foot. I suppose that his weight must have been going on the right side all the time. It makes you wonder just how many runs he might have scored had he been fully fit throughout his career. The mind boggles. I played on the left wing for Tottenham before the war, but I decided to give up the game because I knew it was asking too much of my limbs. If Denis had played less football, cricket would have benefited."

The knee started to give constant pain in 1954 after Compo had blazed to his highest Test score of 278 in just 290 minutes against Pakistan at Trent Bridge. When the England tourists set sail for Australia in the winter for the Ashes series he stayed behind for daily treatment on the knee at Charing Cross Hospital, and followed them out a month later by aircraft. It was a harrowing seven-day stop-and-start flight that he thought was going to cost him his life. Coming in to land for a fuelling stop-over at Karachi, the pilot found that he could not put down the nose wheel of the giant Constellation and he had to crash-land the plane.

Scariest moment
DENIS COMPTON: "It was the scariest moment of my life. There were several unaccompanied children on the flight, and each adult took one on his lap as we came in to land. We had been told exactly what the problem was and knew it was going to be quite bumpy. The pilot did a brilliant job, gliding that monster of a plane in. We landed with a shower of sparks as it lurched and scraped along the runway. The emergency doors had been flung open and I recall acres of sand flying into the cabin. I could not wait to get off for a very large whisky that I drank with shaking hands. The next morning our flight engineer was studying the damage when the plane tilted over and crushed him to death. It was a complete nightmare."

The long sleep

BILL EDRICH: "Denis looked a wreck when we picked him up at Adelaide airport. He had gone seven days since leaving London with only a few hours of sleep. Godders and I got a few drinks down him and then tucked him up in bed at the hotel and he slept through the next twenty-four hours. When he woke up, skipper Len Hutton was sitting by his bed asking if he fancied playing that day."

Getting rid of the rustiness

SIR LEN HUTTON: "I thought that it would be a good idea for Denis to dive straight into action to get rid of the rustiness, and I was also keen to see how fit he was after all his knee problems. He batted against South Australia and scored a century in the first innings. It was remarkable when you think of all the traumas of his flight out to join us."

The Knee briefly took a back seat to The Finger during the first Test. Chasing a ball to the boundary, Denis collided with the fence and broke a finger. He was out of action for a month during which England lost the first Test by an innings and 154 runs and won the second by 38 runs. He returned for the third Test in Melbourne that became known as Tyson's Match. After being knocked unconscious by a Ray Lindwall bouncer, Frank "Typhoon" Tyson recovered to give Australia a taste of their own medicine, skittling them to defeat with seven for 27 in the second innings.

Missing hero

DENIS COMPTON: "Frank Tyson was the most frightening bowler I ever faced in the nets. He just did not seem to know how to bowl within himself, and used to hurl down thunderbolts all the time. First time I saw him bowl was for Northants in that match when he fractured Bill Edrich's cheekbone with a bouncer. While facing him in the nets in Australia he hit me over the heart with one delivery just before the Melbourne Test, and I carried the bruise for the rest of the tour. I knew that if he could find this sort of pace in the Tests the Aussies would be in big trouble. He was knocked all over the place in the first Test, found a good line and length in the second and then murdered 'em in Melbourne. When Ray Lindwall felled him with a fearful bouncer, I said to myself, 'You'll wish you hadn't done that, Lindy.' Sure enough Tyson seemed to double his speed when it came his turn to bowl. Godders was having to stand so far back him that he was almost in the next state! My memory of Frank apart from his speed is of the day we lost him. We got through a lot of bottles of bubbly after clinching the Ashes with a victory in the fourth Test in Adelaide. This, after all, was England's first rubber victory in Australia since the Bodyline tour of 1932-3. It was a long, wild party that started at the ground, continued at the hotel and finished somewhere on the outskirts of Adelaide at a friend's house. As daylight arrived we realised Frank was missing. He had come with us to the house but now nobody could find him. Somebody suggested he might have wandered off into the bush, which really had us worried. We were just organising a search party when we heard a loud snoring sound coming from the lounge. We found our hero flat out underneath the sofa."

Denis was getting twinges of pain in his knee again, and he elected to miss the New Zealand stretch of the tour. He passed the 5,000 Test runs milestone during the following summer series against South Africa, but his old knee trouble flared up in the final Test at the Oval. Denis was batting with new England skipper Peter May when his right knee suddenly gave way as he turned for a run. He was in obvious agony as he hobbled between the wickets.

Tremendously gutsy
PETER MAY: "I tried to persuade Denis that he should have a runner, but he laughed and said, 'That would be too

127

confusing for my poor old brain. I have enough trouble deciding whether to run or not as it is without advising somebody else.' He battled on valiantly and we put on sixty-two runs. Later in the dressing-room I looked at his knee, and it was swollen to twice its normal size. It was only then I appreciated just what sort of pain he must have been in. Denis was not only a quite exceptional batsman, but also a very courageous one."

The only answer
OSMOND CLARKE, orthopaedic surgeon: "Bill Tucker called me in for a second opinion on the knee, and we both agreed that the only answer to the problem was to remove the patella [kneecap]. This way we could at least possibly get Denis playing again. It had reached the point where he could not bend the knee at all, and the pain he was suffering was quite excruciating. Without the operation, Denis accepted that his career would be over. With the operation, the odds were just in favour that he would be able to play on. After thinking about it for a few days, he gave us permission to go ahead and operate."

Compo was admitted to University College Hospital where by sad coincidence his old Arsenal manager Tom Whittaker was battling against an illness from which he would shortly die. It was the winter of 1955. E.M. (Lyn) Wellings, then the London *Evening News* cricket correspondent, was convinced that Denis's career was finished following a tip-off from a contact at the hospital. I was a young sportsroom assistant at the *News*, and was seconded to Wellings to help him put together a "Farewell Compo" supplement. This is when I first started the in-depth research that ultimately led to this book!

Under the supervision of the whip-cracking Wellings, I dug out scores of stories and quotes from *Evening News* files going back to Compo's first appearances with Middlesex and

England. I was then instructed to go to the offices of the *Hendon Times* to scour through early 1930s editions for facts about Compo's schoolboy performances.

An eight-page supplement was ready to go to press when it was announced that the operation had been a success and that Denis had his eye on a comeback against the 1956 Aussies. The "obituaries" on Compo's career were hastily reworded, and the main headline changed to "Welcome Back Compo!"

The most memorable thing for me about that period is being taken by Wellings to meet Sir Jack Hobbs in his Fleet Street sports shop, and listening to his assessment of my hero.

"Greatest since C.B. Fry"

SIR JACK HOBBS: "Denis has provided us all with such wonderful entertainment that it would be quite tragic if his knee forces an early retirement from a game to which he still has so much to give. I scored ninety-seven of my centuries after the age of 40, and would like to think that Denis has still an awful lot of runs left in him. He put too much physical strain on his limbs with all his football, and now I am afraid he is paying the price for simply being too talented a young man. I would say that he is probably the most naturally gifted all-round sportsman this country has produced since C.B. Fry. I have watched him closely from his earliest days, and have enjoyed every moment. He does things that I would never have dreamed of doing. That sweep of his and the late cut are extremely risky strokes, yet he has turned them into works of art. What impresses me most of all is the way he plays off his back foot with such power and confidence. It takes a tremendous eye and quick reflexes, and also a lot of nerve when the likes of Lindwall and Miller are bowling flat out at you. He is also one of the finest players of spin bowling I have seen in a long, long time. I like the way he sets out to dominate the spinners by going down the wicket to them, but again it is a very risky style that I would not recommend to young players setting out to learn how to play the game. Denis has been kind enough to tell me that I was his hero. Well, take it from me, we have a mutual admiration for each other."

A major feature in the "Farewell Comp"' ... "Welcome Back Compo" supplement focused on the most remarkable of all the innings compiled by Denis. It came in South Africa, and those lucky enough to witness it described it as one of the most astonishing innings ever played ...

12: Butcher of Benoni

This was the greatest innings I never saw.
John Arlott

BENONI, South Africa, Saturday 4 December 1948: Denis Compton, playing for the MCC tourists, today hit the fastest triple century in the history of first-class cricket. He reached 300 against North-eastern Transvaal in just 181 minutes during a third-wicket stand of 399 with Notts opener Reg Simpson (130 not out). Compton scored 198 of his runs in boundaries, with 5 sixes and 42 fours. He raced to his first century in 66 minutes, his second in 79 minutes and his third in just 37 minutes.

Reuters News Agency

Extravagant shots

REG HAYTER, London agency journalist who was reporting on the spot at Benoni: "I could hardly keep up with Denis making my notes, and the scoreboard was often several runs behind. There has never been an innings quite like it. He was walking down the wicket even before the bowler released the ball, and made his runs with an astonishing array of extravagant shots. Denis was never one for statistics, and did not have any record in mind. He was just out there enjoying himself, and the crowd loved every second of it. There was a stand at long on packed with black spectators, and they roared when Denis hit a six over their stand. 'Give us another one, massah Denis,' they chanted, and Denis quickly obliged. It was just unbelievable, and I felt privileged to be there to report it."

I need to detour here to give the background as to how I got the inside facts for this chapter because it involves an amusing story about my good pal Jimmy Greaves. The late Reg Hayter was a legendary Fleet Street sports agency boss who was a lifelong friend, mentor, drinking partner, soul mate and loyal protector of Compo. His son, Peter, is the highly respected cricket correspondent for the *Mail on Sunday*.

Reg and trusted members of his renowned Hayters Agency ghosted and/or edited many of the articles and books that appeared under the Compton by-line. He and the then *Sun* sports editor Frank Nicklin ran a team of golden oldies that played charity cricket matches around the country. I volunteered the services of Jimmy Greaves for a match in deepest Derbyshire.

Greavsie had only recently won his well-publicised battle against the curse of alcoholism, and I convinced him that a day out in Derbyshire would do him the world of good. He had been a County-class cricketer when a young professional footballer with Chelsea, and would have combined both sports *à la* Compton but for an order from his club manager Ted Drake that he had to concentrate 100 per cent on football. Over to Greavsie ...

Greavsie ducks out
JIMMY GREAVES: "Against my better judgement, I made the seven-hour 400-mile round trip with Norman from my Essex home, leaving at the crack of dawn. It was my first game of cricket for years. I batted at number six, didn't get a sniff of the ball and was out for a golden duck as my stumps

were flattened. Dropping Norman off in London that evening, I got involved in a slanging match and near-fisticuffs with a bus driver who cut me up and scraped right along the side of my new car. I was not a happy bunny. The following week I received a local Derbyshire newspaper in the post from that old rascal Frank Nicklin that had a thick headline going across seven columns on the back page: 'Greaves Flops With First Ball Duck.' It was a bigger headline than I ever got during my football career."

You will understand just why this anecdote is included in the chapter on Compo's fantastic triple century when I tell you that opening the batting for the Hayter/Nicklin golden oldies team was none other than Reg Simpson, who had the best view of all of the record-making knock in Benoni. The former Nottinghamshire and England opening master, one of the finest players of fast bowling there has ever been, described Compo's innings like a man recalling a pleasant dream.

Barrage of boundaries

REG SIMPSON: "It was quite unreal. I just concentrated on keeping my wicket intact so that I could stay out there and watch. It's fair to say that the bowling was not anywhere near Test-match standard, and the ground was on the small side. Even so, what Denis did that afternoon was just extraordinary. They had three good-class bowlers, who Denis saw off with a barrage of boundaries. Then their captain tried all sorts of permutations in an effort to contain him, but this was a day when nobody could have tied Denis down. At times he was so far down the wicket to the spinners that I could almost have reached out and shaken his hand. In desperation the captain ordered everybody but the bowler and wicket-keeper to patrol the boundaries. Still Denis penetrated the field with shots that flashed to all points. At one stage his right hand slipped off the handle, and he swatted the ball one-handed for six as if lobbing a shot on the centre court at Wimbledon. It was like batting with a man with a machine gun, and the South Africans were just reduced to collecting rather than fielding the ball. Nobody has scored a faster 300 to this day, and if Denis had put his mind to it he could have scored many more, but he just surrendered his wicket once the 300 was on the board. John Arlott has always described it as the greatest innings he never saw."

The Big Sleep

JOHN ARLOTT: "I was dog tired when I arrived in Johannesburg after a long flight on the morning of the match. As I was checking into my room I bumped into Bill Ferguson, MCC's long-serving baggage man. He had come back to the hotel to collect some equipment and a taxi was waiting for him. 'Going to join me?' he asked. I was about to take him up on his offer when I saw before me a vision of a hot bath and a freshly made bed. What was a meaningless match in Benoni when compared with the luxury of sleep? I satisfied myself that I would give the tour my full concentration in time for the first Test in Durban ten days later. For now, all I wanted to do was sleep. I slept the sleep of Rip Van Winkle and awoke twenty hours later to be gleefully informed of the phenomenal Compton innings. Yes, it was indeed the greatest innings I never saw. I never again turned down the opportunity to go to any cricket match. You just never know."

Eamonn Andrews instructed me to invite John Arlott to come on the *This Is Your Life* tribute show to Denis to tell the story of how he missed Compo's remarkable triple century, but he refused point blank. "I detest the show, and see it as an invasion of privacy," he told me, and he had in fact previously blocked several attempts by Eamonn to make him a subject for the Big Red Book. Arlott added in that unmistakable

Hampshire burr of his, "Anyway, I would be the last person Denis would want to see coming through the doors. My admiration for him begins and ends with his undeniable talent as a genius of a batsman. He brought great fun to cricket, and for that all of us whose summers he brightened will always be grateful." I tried to draw Denis on the reasons behind this feud with Arlott, but he just shrugged and said, "Just let's say we would not be each other's first choice for company on a desert island." The root of their differences lay in their opposite views on the subject of South African politics, and neither would cross the bridge to meet the other halfway. When England played Australia in the Centenary Test in 1977, there were strong rumours that Bill Edrich had taken up the argument with Arlott during a "golden oldies" flight out from London. The story flashed around that the famous broadcaster had given the famous ex-cricketer a black eye with an angrily aimed punch. Sure enough, when Edrich arrived in Oz he was sporting a painful shiner. Peter Watson, then sports editor on the London *Evening News* and later executive sports chief and hard-hitting columnist on the *Sunday Express*, saw the incident on the plane from close quarters and gave me the following account of exactly what happened.

A thump in the eye
PETER WATSON: "Bill seemed to be flying higher than the plane even before we took off from Heathrow. Champers flowed throughout the flight and Bill, always the life and soul of any party, became rowdier and rowdier. He was walking up and down the aisle trying to get us all to join in a sing-song. John Arlott was dozing in his seat just across the aisle from me. He had fallen asleep with his headphones on and was tuned into a classical music tape. Bill stopped alongside him and turned the volume up to full pitch. Arlott nearly jumped out of his seat, and lashed out – perhaps deliberately or purely instinctively – and thumped Bill right

135

in the eye. It was all over in seconds, and not a fist fight as was reported in some quarters. What I found very touching was the way Denis took command of the situation. He guided the worse for wear Edrich to the toilet and cleaned him up, then led him back to his seat and instructed him to get some sleep. When he woke up his eye was swollen and bloodshot. Denis looked after him like a brother right the way through that memorable trip to Melbourne. It really showed Compo's caring side."

Treated like a king

BILL EDRICH: "I could not tell you too much about the flight out to Melbourne. You could say that I was in a party mood even before I got on board. I had been celebrating Denis managing to make the flight. He arrived at Heathrow without his passport, and it was only a fast-driving friend bringing it from a hotel in Wales where he had left it that enabled him to catch the plane. What I do know is that I had ten of the greatest days of my life meeting up with old friends both from my cricketing and my RAF days. When we landed at Melbourne everybody wanted to know about my shiner, but I just laughed it off. You would not believe the reception we got, particularly Denis. They loved him out there almost as much as at home, but the place where he was really treated like a king was South Africa. They still talk about that 300 of his. He had an incredible tour, and averaged well over a hundred. You would think they would have been glad to see the back of him, but he used to get receptions going to and from the wicket as if he was one of theirs. I think that Denis had the sunshine of South Africa in his heart."

Cry freedom

DENIS COMPTON: "I was just set on having some fun in Benoni, and to be honest I enjoyed outrageous good fortune. I could have been out several times as I danced down the wicket to just about every ball that came at me. I knew I was scoring pretty quickly, but had no idea that I was setting a world record. I have always thought that Reg Simpson did not get nearly enough credit for the way he kept unselfishly seeing to it that I had strike. Once I had passed 200 I was quite happy to get out and let somebody else have some batting practice. But it was one of those days when I just could not miss the ball, and it kept flying to the boundary. It was my lovely old pal Reg Hayter who told me exactly what I had achieved. He was a bit of a stutterer at the best of times, and could hardly get the words out as he told me I had scored the fastest 300 on record. We had a lot of bubbly that night, on Reg as I remember. The lovely people of Benoni overwhelmed me with their generosity of spirit. I had knocked their bowlers all over the field, and they rewarded me with the freedom of the town. Whenever I visited South Africa after that the Mayor of Benoni always made a point of contacting me and inviting me down for a civic reception."

Perfect role model
JIMMY GREAVES: "Like most boys from my generation, I wanted to be Denis Compton when I was a kid playing in the street. He awoke the sporting ambitions in thousands of youngsters, and showed that both cricket and football could not only be combined but played with a smile. He was the most perfect role model a boy could ask for, and I should not think any British sportsman before or since has given so many people so much pleasure and enjoyment. We shared the same agent, and so we got to know each other well. There wasn't a boastful bone in his body, and he never fell into the old sportsman's trap of always living in the past and knocking all things modern. I had some enjoyable social times with Denis, and found him a real charmer. The only thing I could never get out of him was a satisfactory explanation for **his** famous black eye!"

13: Black-eye Drama

At his best, there were few who could
match Denis for producing shots
that were purely instinctive.
Sir Donald Bradman

THE Compton Knee was briefly overtaken as a subject for excited national debate by the Compton Black Eye during the 1950-1 Ashes series in Australia. It was the most miserable time of Compo's career. He was vice-captain to Freddie Brown, and the weight of responsibility when added to his painful knee problem and a pending divorce from his first wife led to a disastrous loss of form and confidence. One of the greatest runmakers of all time stumbled through a Test series with scores of 3, 0, 0, 23, 5, 0, 11 and 11 not out for an aggregate 53 and an almost unbelievable average 7.57. A sensation-seeking journalist on the tour suggested that Denis was paying the price for being a playboy off the field, and Compo inadvertently fuelled the rumour machine by getting himself a nasty black eye.

Stitched wound
DENIS COMPTON: "I was at a late evening Christmas-time garden party at the Melbourne home of a golfing friend of mine, Bill Gluth. While sitting at a table I turned my head quickly and gashed my eyebrow on a garden tap jutting out

from a wall. It sounds improbable, but that's what happened. A doctor was called and I had to have several stitches inserted. The eye became very swollen and it looked for all the world as if I had been punched by Rocky Marciano. Because of the injury, I arrived a day later than the rest of the team for the third Test in Sydney and had dark glasses covering my eyes in an effort to hide the damage. I knew that if the press saw it they would put two and two together and make five."

Compo's fears were well founded. A photographer for the *Sydney Sun* snatched a picture of Compo without his dark glasses in his hotel room, and the story circulated that he had been punched by an irate husband. This later became embellished to take in the storyline that he had been shinning down a drainpipe from a bedroom window when spotted by the husband. The picture was used as evidence of Compo's misconduct off the field.

Few believed the garden tap story, but more than thirty years on he was sticking to it. Part of me wanted to believe the whispers about his swashbuckling lifestyle, but he refused to budge on the reported facts, although the smile playing at the side of his lips suggested there was more to it than, so to speak, met the eye. Much more worrying to Denis than the unfounded rumours was his complete collapse of form. It was so big a personal crisis that he went to the top of the mountain for help and advice. He contacted Don Bradman, who was into his third year of retirement after the greatest of all Test careers in which he averaged a mind-boggling 99.94.

A bedroom lesson
SIR DONALD BRADMAN: "Denis had hit an atrocious run of form. He came to see me at the hotel in Melbourne where I was staying and we discussed what he was doing wrong. Denis had always been a creature of impulse and invention,

but had lost confidence to the point where he was no longer doing what came naturally. At his best, there were few who could match him for producing shots at the wicket that were purely instinctive and of his own making. Suddenly, as happens to all batsmen at some stage in their career, his form had deserted him. I just happened to have a cricket bat in my hotel bedroom, and for ten minutes I gave a demonstration of the way he was batting and the way that I considered he could improve his shots and his footwork."

Masterclass from The Don
DENIS COMPTON: "It was wonderfully generous of The Don to give me his time and wisdom. It truly was a masterclass. I told him that I felt as if I was suddenly batting with a stump rather than a bat. He gave me a demonstration of stroke play and footwork against an imaginary bowler, and showed how I was getting my feet in the wrong position and playing across the line. I wish I could say that The Don's magic had rubbed off on me. But if anything, it made me worse. I had never in my career had to think deeply about what I was doing at the crease. Suddenly, I was thinking too much and just getting in a right old tangle.

Things had not always been that cordial between The Don and Denis on the field of play. On the previous tour of Australia in 1946-7 there had been an undercurrent of anger when Bradman refused to walk after what the England fielders were convinced was a good catch by Jack Ikin at second slip off the bowling of Bill Voce. The Don was 28 at the time, and went on to make a match-winning 187.

Angry skipper
DENIS COMPTON: "None of us was in any doubt that Don had got a snick, but the umpire gave it not out. Most of us shrugged and got on with the game, but I recall that our skipper Wally Hammond was absolutely livid. He hardly

spoke a civil word to The Don for the rest of the tour, apart from saying heads or tails when they tossed up. Then, in the Adelaide Test, The Don became extremely frustrated at the way I was playing. It was during my stand with Godfrey Evans when Godders went a record ninety-seven minutes without scoring while I farmed the bowling."

Invitation to run

GODFREY EVANS: "The Don was placing his fielders around the boundary inviting Denis to take singles or threes in a bid to get me on strike. But Compo would have none of it and just kept taking twos, boundaries and end-of-over singles to keep the batting. He kept refusing runs on his way to his second century of the match, and The Don was not at all happy about it."

Win at all costs

DENIS COMPTON: "At the end of one over, Don said to me, 'This is not the way to play cricket.' I replied, 'You set a proper field, and I'll play proper cricket.' Then he complained to the umpire that I was scuffing up the pitch when going down the wicket to spinner Colin McCool. 'We've got to bat on that when you're finished,' he said to me tersely. I laughed and said, 'Would you rather me take off my boots?' Don was the king as far as I was concerned but there was a win-at-all-costs streak in him that could turn him into a less than likeable opponent. I suppose it was one of the qualities that helped make him such an outstanding batsman. He just did not like to be beaten. We never fell out over it, and I was honoured to be the only Englishman invited to his eighty-fifth birthday party in 1993."

It was on the 1950-1 tour of Australia that Compo's form and luck was at an all-time low, and even Bradman's coaching could not dig him out of his black hole of despair. By the time of the fourth Test in Adelaide his famous jaunty walk had become a slow limp as the condition of his knee continued to worsen. Even his many pals in the Australian team were beginning to feel sorry for him. He went for five, caught behind by Don Tallon off the bowling of Ray Lindwall in the first innings. As he walked past his good friend Bill Johnston for the start of his second innings, he got a surprise offer of a free run.

One off the mark

DENIS COMPTON: "Bill whispered out of the side of his mouth, 'You poor old cobber. Don't worry, I'll give you one to get you off the mark.' True to his word, Bill bowled me a dolly first ball that was begging to be hit to the boundary. I middled it perfectly and watched in horror as the ball flew straight into the hands of substitute fielder Sam Loxton at midwicket! I could not even get runs with the help of the bowler. That was the only time I was ever offered a free ball, and I messed it up. It was not the greatest time in my life."

There was much better to come against the Aussies. Two years later it was Compo who hit the winning run to clinch the historic Ashes victory for England at the Oval. It ended a record drought of 18 years 362 days without an Ashes triumph.

An indication of the way the series grabbed the nation's attention is that an all-time record aggregate of 550,000 spectators watched the five matches. A Hollywood scriptwriter could not have invented a more memorable or emotional climax to the series. There were forty-four runs needed for victory – for the Ashes – when Denis walked to the wicket. Waiting for him in the middle was Bill Edrich. The Terrible Twins together against the old enemy.

They went about getting the runs in a workmanlike rather than stylish manner. The Australians made them battle for every run, until skipper Lindsay Hassett finally conceded the game was lost. With four runs needed, he put on non-bowler

Arthur Morris for the last rites. Denis was on strike, with his faithful partner watching and waiting at the other end.

Unforgettable moment
DENIS COMPTON: "Every cricket lover knew the significance of Arthur taking the ball. It signalled that the Australians had accepted that the Ashes were ours. I managed to find the boundary off Arthur's fifth ball to clinch victory. Bill and I crossed as the ball flew away and he was whooping like a boy opening his presents on Christmas morning. Edrich and Compton together. It was an unforgettable moment for the two of us. Our hardest job was getting back to the dressing-room. We were mobbed as we ran back to the pavilion, and then the party really started."

Champagne moment
BILL EDRICH: "We had waited a long time for that celebration, and, boy, did we celebrate. The champagne was coming out of our ears. Denis and I had dreamed of this moment from when we first started out as lads at Lord's, and we deserved that drink! The Australians came into our dressing-room to join in the party and helped us literally shift the bottles. Keith Miller tossed an empty one out of the window and that started a throwing match."

The stopped clock
KEITH MILLER: "We were drowning our sorrows, but were happy for the England boys. Let's face it, they had been thirsting for this success for years. As I recall, one of the flying champagne bottles struck the dressing-room clock and stopped it at what was an historic time for English cricket. It was one helluva party, and it continued long into the night."

Happy hangover
DENIS COMPTON: "I have only a hazy recollection of what happened after we left the Oval. We went on the town and

143

just everywhere people were queuing up to pat us on the back and buy us drinks. I woke up the next morning in a friend's flat with an almighty hangover. But I had rarely felt happier in my life! You needed to be around at that time to realise the impact our Ashes victory made. It was the summer of the Queen's Coronation, Everest being conquered for the first time and Gordon Richards winning his one and only Derby in the week that he was knighted. The euphoria over our Ashes victory was just unbelievable, and for weeks afterwards we were all walking on air. It was one of the most memorable times of my life."

14: The Final Runs

There was not one of us in the Australian side that was not sad to see the back of Denis for the last time.
Neil Harvey

THERE were still four more years to be added to Compo's seventy-eight-match Test career after the 1953 Ashes triumph, but he was taking a painful path towards retirement. It was The Knee, minus the cap, that forced Denis to shoulder his bat at the age of thirty-nine. His famous nautical-roll walk had been reduced to a limp, but he was still able to contribute a century – the 123rd of his glorious career – to his final game for Middlesex against Worcestershire at his beloved Lord's in August 1957.

A year earlier I had seen Denis play just some of his shots in his final Test in England against the old enemy Australia. I was summoned to Lord's to telephone in Len Hutton's copy in my role as a sportsroom assistant on the London *Evening News*. Hutton had been hired by the *News* as a guest reporter. E.M. (Lyn) Wellings, the paper's highly respected but extremely tetchy cricket correspondent, objected to the appointment at a time when a storm was brewing in Fleet Street over the employment of non-journalist sportswriters.

Right up to the close of his distinguished reporting career, Wellings kept up a campaign to guard the press box against interlopers. He was firmly of the opinion that it should be the domain only of *bona fide* cricket writers. One of the things that used to irk him was when the BBC Television cameras would pan the press box during a Test match. He saw this as a gross invasion of privacy. Hence, during one such lingering look into the press box at Lord's, the television director was jolted into a quick cut when he saw on his monitor Wellings holding up a foolscap page in front of his face that had printed on it in large, unmissable letters the word, "BOLLOCKS!"

Anyway, returning to the Oval Test in 1956: Wellings kicked up such a fuss that he succeeded in getting Hutton – the newly knighted Sir Leonard – barred from the press box. The recently retired England captain suffered the indignity of being forced to sit outside next to his ghostwriter, Julian Holland (later editor of radio's *News at One*). Wellings flatly refused to let me use his press-box telephone and I had to keep running to a public call box at the back of the main stand to dictate the copy, which explains why I did not see all of Compo's shots. It was a dashing old-style knock of ninety-four that no less a person than Sir Don Bradman described as the best innings of the series.

I stood up watching most of his runs. My seat had been "stolen" by an *Evening News* reporter recently returned from Army National Service in Malaya. It was Leslie Thomas, who was taking time off from penning a novel called *Virgin Soldiers*. Leslie, a keen Lord's Taverner, was at Westminster Abbey for the Thanksgiving Service.

Heartbreaking

LESLIE THOMAS: "I started my National Service in 1949 when Denis's popularity was at its peak. We were all Compo disciples out in Malaya and could not wait to get news of his latest innings. That knock of ninety-four of his against Australia must measure up to his very best because he achieved it on virtually one leg. It was heartbreaking when he failed to get his hundred by six runs because we all knew in our hearts that this would be Compo's last stand against the old enemy. He gave me so much pleasure during his lifetime that I just had to be here at Westminster Abbey to say a fond farewell. He was a hero of heroes."

Knights at the Savoy

DENIS COMPTON: "Immediately after my ninety-four, I hurried back to the dressing-room and got bathed and changed for a private black-tie dinner at the Savoy where the Prime Minister of Australia, Robert Menzies, was the guest of honour along with great cricketing knights Sir Don Bradman, Sir Jack Hobbs, Sir Pelham Warner and Sir Len Hutton. I read Len's article in the *Evening News* on the way to the hotel in a cab, and noticed that he was very grudging in his praise and wrote that in his opinion he did not think I should have been recalled to the team because of the doubts about my fitness. He said to me over dinner that he could not understand why I should want to play when it was so obviously such hard work. I told him that I had enjoyed every minute of my innings, but I'm not sure he believed me. Len and I had different views as to what amounted to enjoyment on a cricket field."

A typical gem

SIR LEN HUTTON: "I remember that E.M. Wellings refused to acknowledge my presence at the Oval. It became commonplace for retired sportsmen to take up careers in journalism, but back in 1956 it was fairly novel and caused a bit of a stir. The editor of the *News* at the time was a cricket-daft Yorkshireman called Reg Willis, whom I had known for years. He was determined that my views should appear in his paper regardless of what Mr. Wellings thought. My comment that Denis should not have been considered for the Test against Australia came out much harsher than I meant it. The point I was making was that he needed longer to get over having his kneecap removed. The bulk of the *Evening News* article that annoyed Denis so much was written before he started his knock, and he was still in full swing when the last edition went to press. So my reporting of his performance was mixed in with comments that I had made before he reached the wicket. When Denis later became a full-time journalist I think he better understood the position I had been in. His innings of ninety-four was a typical Compton gem, and I don't know how he managed it with such a handicap. And yes, Denis did seem to enjoy every minute of it despite having only one kneecap. Anybody else would have found it hard work."

Written off

KEITH MILLER: "That Oval Test was the last one in which Denis and I played against each other. I very nearly spoiled the old boy's comeback by bowling him first ball. It was just a whisker away from knocking his off stump flying. Then he put together an innings of great beauty during which he reached back into the past and played some of those glorious shots that only he could play. It was an incredible knock when you consider that he had been written off as finished following the removal of his kneecap. I contacted him in hospital when he was in for the operation and he told me defiantly that he would see me in the next Test series, but I'm not sure that either of us really believed this. It was as much a thrill for us tourists as for the England supporters when it was announced that Compo was being recalled for the final Test at the Oval. What a treat he gave everybody, even though a lot of his movement was restricted by that capless knee of his. I know I speak for all the Aussies on the field of play that day when I say that we were genuinely sorry that he did not quite make his century. In the second innings he had scored thirty-odd not out when England declared, and we clapped him all the way back to the pavilion as if he had scored a century. Denis gave me a significant nod and wave of the bat. Both of us knew we would never see each other at opposite ends of a Test pitch again and it was all very emotional. The man was something very special."

Favourite opponent

NEIL HARVEY, Australia's left-hand batting artist: "There was not one of us in the Australian side that was not sad to see the back of Denis for the last time. He was our favourite opponent, not only because of the way he played the game but because of his great sportsmanship on and off the field. He was always the first into the dressing-room to congratulate us on a victory or a good knock. When we applauded as Alan Davidson caught him off the bowling of Ron Archer in that first innings it was not at the fall of his wicket but in appreciation of a master at work. It was a magnificent knock, and deserved to be a century. I was in awe of Denis when I first broke into the Australian team in 1948, and was too shy really to get to know him. But in later years I found out just why Keith Miller and he were such soul mates. They had the same outlook on life and on cricket. I went to Ireland quite a few years after I retired, and who should I bump into there but the lovely Compo. We had a great time together talking about old times, and I was delighted to get the chance to tell him to his face that I reckoned he was one of the greatest batsmen it had ever been my pleasure to field against. Something was always happening when Denis was at the wicket, and that last big innings of his against us captured what his batting had been all about. He was a great entertainer and a great bloke."

Compo's contribution of 94 and 35 not out against the Australians in that Oval Test clinched a place for him in the England squad to tour his favourite hunting ground of South Africa in 1956-57. He did not set the world alight in the five Tests of his swansong series, scoring 6, 32, 58, 64, 16, 19,

42, 1, 0 and 5. It was the series in which Hugh "Toey" Tayfield tied England down with his naggingly accurate off spin and finished with a South African record haul of thirty-seven wickets. The old Compton would have been down the wicket taking on Tayfield, but the knee handicap made him a prisoner of his crease.

Painful decision

DENIS COMPTON: "Toey Tayfield and Trevor Goddard exposed the fact that I lacked any sort of mobility. I knew what I wanted to do but could not get my feet moving to produce the sort of shots that had served me so well in the past. My footwork was as important to me as what I did with the bat. It was painfully obvious to me that I was going to have to bow out of cricket. I confided in our skipper Peter May that this would be my last Test series and he said, 'I think you are wise. You are asking too much of that knee of yours.' Peter had seen at close quarters the sort of pain I was quietly suffering, and I knew he was right with his assessment."

Godfather May

PETER MAY: "Denis told me confidentially about his retirement decision on the day I was godfather at the christening of his son, Richard, at the magnificent home of his South African wife at the time, Valerie. I was almost relieved to hear him say that he was going to make it his last series because I knew better than anybody the torture he was putting himself through every time he went to the wicket. Denis had been one of my heroes when I was first making my way as a batsman, and it was sad to see him struggling to reproduce his magical touch. He had put a lot of sparkle into cricket both with his performances and his personality, and I think that everybody wanted to remember him the way he was rather than watch him scrambling for runs. At his peak, he was one of the Great Untouchables."

Peter May was a guest on Compo's *This Is Your Life* tribute show. Denis was thrilled to see him, not only because he was an old personal friend but because he rated him the finest batsman of his generation. Unfortunately, because of pressures of the clock, the contribution Peter was going to make to the programme was squeezed out. Peter had been elected spokesman for an array of his old cricketing chums including Fred Trueman, Godfrey Evans, Alec Bedser, Trevor Bailey, Ted Dexter, John Warr, Don Wilson, Alan Oakman, Fred Rumsey, Colin Milburn, Colin Ingleby-Mackenzie and Doug Insole. The following is what Peter agreed he would say had Eamonn had the time to go to him on the *This Is Your Life* set.

Natural-born genius

PETER MAY: "Denis brought sunshine into all our lives in the dark days of austerity immediately after the war. I was one of many cricketers inspired not only by his dazzling displays with the bat but his cavalier approach to cricket and life. Those of us who wanted to bat the Compton way quickly realised that his style was quite unique to him. Nobody could be coached to play like that. He was a natural-born genius. I have to say he had his faults. You could never set your clock by Denis, and he was as forgetful as an absent-minded professor. But he had the sort of disarming charm that melted any annoyance over his late arrivals or his forgotten equipment. It was a privilege to play with him and a joy to have had him as a friend. His fame transcended the great game of ours, but it never went to that Brylcreemed head of his. On behalf of everybody in cricket, Denis, I salute you and thank you for all the entertainment you gave to millions of people."

It was fitting that when Denis played his final innings his partner at the other end of the pitch was his "twin" Bill Edrich, who was skippering Middlesex against Worcestershire at

Lord's in the final weekend of August 1957. It was twenty–two years and more than 75,000 runs since they had started off together with a match-winning last-wicket stand for the MCC team at Beaumont College. Both of them, Denis in particular, had put on a lot of pounds since their days as the young lions of English cricket and there was now more of a trot than a gallop to their game. Lord's was packed with supporters wanting to see the maestro's final runs. They were not disappointed. Denis scored a century in the first innings against Worcestershire and had reached forty-eight in the second innings when he lost his wicket for the last time in spectacular fashion.

The last shot
BILL EDRICH: "Denis was full of intent, and I knew that he wanted to go out with a second century in the match. Worcester off-break bowler Martin Horton flighted the ball invitingly to him. Denis opened his shoulders and went for a big hit. The ball sailed away and the crowd was on its feet cheering him reaching his half-century with a six. The cheers turned to groans as a Ceylon-born outfielder with the unlikely name of Ladislaw Outschoorn spoiled the party by catching the ball at the second attempt out on the boundary. Denis laughed, waved his bat to me and set off for the pavilion for the last time. The crowd quickly recovered from the disappointment of the catch and cheered him as if he had just won the Ashes ... again. He could not have stage-managed a better exit. I don't mind admitting that I had a lump in my throat the size of a boulder. Boy, did we have a good drink that night."

Prized wicket
MARTIN HORTON: "I was almost sad to take Denis's wicket, but at least he perished in style somewhere down by the boundary. I will eat out on this moment for years to come. I was the last man to take the great Denis Compton's wicket!

What a prize. It's doubtful we shall see a batsman like him again."

This sporting life

DENIS COMPTON: "In a perfect world I would have liked to play on for another ten or more years. Sadly, the knee was just not up to it. But how could I complain? I'd had a wonderful career, travelled the world, made great friends, been lucky enough to have played both cricket and football at top level and had enjoyed every second of it. I cannot think of anybody who has had a better sporting life. Wish that I could do it all over again. I would not change a thing, apart from make my knee stronger!"

15: Brylcreem Boy

*I saw to it that Denis was able to concentrate
on doing what he did better than anybody
else — and that was to play cricket.*
Bagenal Harvey

THE face of Denis Compton was arguably the best known in Britain during the 1950s. It stared down from billboards, the sides of buses and trams, from railway station and tube train posters, out of newspaper and magazine advertisements and from the wall of just about every barber's shop in the land. His handsome features and well-groomed dark hair were used to promote and advertise Brylcreem. He was the first sportsman launched in such a mammoth nationwide advertising campaign as he became the willing tool of a new phenomenon: the sports agent.

The romantic story circulating for years was that businessman Bagenal Harvey was given a lift from Lord's by Denis, and when he opened the passenger-side door he found hundreds of unanswered letters spilling out. Bagenal, so the story went, told Denis that he would organise replies for all the letters and also take over as his agent. It is a false story that robs his old friend, the late Reg Hayter, of the credit he deserves for putting Compo on the road to riches. This is the true story, as related to me by Reg ...

Packed suitcase
REG HAYTER: "It was round about Christmas time 1948, and I was in South Africa reporting the MCC tour for the Press

154

Association. Denis and I were having a quiet beer or three when he leaned forward in a conspiratorial kind of way and said, 'I've got a suitcase in my room that I'd like you to look at.' It turned out that the case was crammed with hundreds of unopened and unanswered letters. 'What am I going to do?' said Denis. 'I can't possibly answer all of these.' I took the suitcase off him and spent several hours going through all the letters, putting them into priority piles. Many were fan letters, particularly from women and young girls, requesting signed photographs, but also among them were offers for him to open shops, write newspaper and magazine columns, put his name to books and give after-dinner and club talks. I told Denis that I would help him reply to the letters and that when we got back to Blighty I would introduce him to somebody who would advise him how to profit from his off-field activities."

Reg told this tale while padded up waiting to go out to bat in the Derbyshire charity match in which Jimmy Greaves got his famous first-ball duck [see page 132]. His best pal Frank Nicklin, then sports editor of the *Sun*, chipped in with, "Tell them about the day you were mistaken for Denis and almost got a punch on the nose." Just at that moment a wicket fell and it was Reg's turn to bat. "You tell them,' said Reg. "I'll be back in time for the punchline."

Mistaken identity
FRANK NICKLIN: "When he was younger, Reg could have been mistaken as Denis's brother. They were that much alike to look at. As you're about to see, he bats nothing like him. Anyway, one night during a Test match at Old Trafford, Reg was stopped in the hotel corridor by a wealthy England supporter who was nicely cut. 'Denis, old chap,' he said, shaking Reg by the hand, 'just the man I've been looking for. We're having a party in my room and I want you to come and join us.' Reg wanted to protest that he was not Denis

Compton, but you know, with that stutter of his, by the time he got the words out the man had dragged him into the party. A large whisky was placed in Reg's hand, and so he decided he might as well play along and be the man they wanted for a while. He slipped away after half an hour and when he went to his room next door but one he found a very becoming lady about to climb into his bed. She was as naked as the day she was born, and there and then Reg's stutter was almost cured. 'What's going on?' asked Reg, or words to that effect. 'Hello, Denis darling,' she said, 'I've just come to give you a goodnight kiss.' [There was the clattering sound of stumps being hit out in the middle]. Hold on, Reg can tell you the rest of the story. He's just got himself run out. So he does bat like Compo."

The naked lady
REG HAYTER, still in his pads having not bothered the scorer: "It's a true story about the naked lady and me. I was just asking her what she thought she was doing when the door swung open and her irate husband burst in. He grabbed her by the hair and yanked her out of the room. So neither Denis nor I got lucky that night! Anyway, as I was saying before I was so rudely interrupted ... I introduced Denis to Bagenal Harvey when we returned to London. I knew he had a good business head on his shoulders and would know how to make the most of Denis's commercial potential. It was the start of a phenomenally successful venture."

Starting off with Denis, Bagenal Harvey became a master sports agent who set standards that have, sadly, not been met by all the agents who followed his lead. It was the £1,000-a-year nine-year contract with Brylcreem that got both Denis and Bagenal up and running. He did such a spectacular job steering Denis that he was soon attracting the interest of other sportsmen. Quietly and without fuss, the Dublin-born and educated Harvey built up a client list that, speaking in racing terms, was a top thoroughbred stable. Colin Cowdrey, Tom Graveney and Fred Trueman were among cricketers who came under his guidance, and other sporting masters who put their business affairs in his hands included Bobby Charlton, Johnny Haynes, Jimmy Greaves, Lynn Davies, Mary Rand and Owen Davidson. He was the first to realise the commercial potential of media sports commentators and columnists and became affectionately known as the "Unofficial Governor of the BBC" when he started negotiating for the likes of David Coleman, John Arlott, Eddie Waring, Jimmy Hill and Frank Bough. He also steered the All England Club at Wimbledon towards hugely lucrative contracts, and was for many years arguably the most powerful man on the sporting sidelines. The Bagenal Harvey agency later came under the creative stewardship of his long-time loyal right hand man Geoffrey Irvine. Sadly, Bagenal was too ill to come on Compo's *This Is Your Life* show and he died soon after the programme was screened. I once asked him the secret of his success ...

Final decision

BAGENAL HARVEY: "I always leave the final decision to my clients, and take 10 per cent of the fee for doing 90 per cent of the negotiating. I merely recommend what I think is the right deal, and then put the ball in their court. If there is a secret, it is only to handle people with whom you are happy being in the same room. I like to be proud of my client list. There are uncouth agents coming into the world of sport who give our business a bad name with their crude negotiating techniques, and they don't seem to mind who they handle as long as they get their cut. They have turned 'agent' into a dirty word. I prefer to be known as a representative, and I have no desire to be as famous or more famous than my clients. I was very lucky, with Reg Hayter's invaluable help, to start off with Denis. If anybody ever needed a representative, it was him. I know he will not mind me saying that he was one of the most disorganised people on earth when he came to my attention. He really did use the back seat of his car and the boot as filing cabinets. The first time he gave me a lift letters came tumbling out on to the pavement as I opened the car door to get in. As Reg had warned, this was a man in serious need of organisational help. I took all the outside business worries off his shoulders, and this allowed him to concentrate 100per cent on what he did better than anybody else – and that was playing cricket. I had a member of my staff whose one job was to look after Denis. Mind you, even I could never give a guarantee that he would turn up either on time or at the right place. He often had Reg and I tearing out our hair with his forgetfulness. But it was all part of his endearing charm. One thing, Denis was never boring – either on or off the field of play."

Compo's "minder" was an engaging young man called John Shrewsbury, who later became one of the top television sports directors at the BBC and included thirteen FA Cup Finals, Euro96 and the British Open golf coverage in his impressive portfolio. His one disappointment is that he never got to direct the cameras when Denis was blazing the run trail. All we have to remind us of Compo's genius is grainy black and white newsreel footage that does not do justice to the majesty of his batting. John never lost his affection for Compo, despite often being driven to distraction by his foggy attention to detail.

Land of the gods
JOHN SHREWSBURY: "I hero-worshipped Denis when I was a schoolboy, and never found any reason to think less highly of him when I handled his diary. Yes, he was one of the worst time keepers I have ever known and there were occasions when he would forget completely when and where he should be despite repeated reminders. Yet I never knew anybody

who was kept waiting by Denis who did not find the wait well worthwhile when he finally made his appearance. He could charm the birds down out of the trees and then make them sing. All the time I worked with him I never knew him utter one boastful remark about sporting feats that, let's be honest, put him in the land of the gods. Can you imagine how many times they would replay his sweep shots, late cuts and charges up the wicket if there had been today's television technology around in his prime? I think the story that best illustrates the kind of man he was is the day I told him that I had to play in a charity cricket match. He insisted on giving me his boots and a bat. They remain my most treasured reminders of a lovely, warm generous person and a cricketing legend."

When he hung up his bat for the last time, Denis became a successful contacts man for Royds and then the McCann Ericson advertising agency. Long after his final runs his name on an invitation card pulled in high-powered businessmen who wanted to meet The Legend. They were never disappointed, and Denis steered a lot of contracts into the McCann Ericson net. He was also a cricket columnist with the *Sunday Express* and a commentator with BBC Television. The only bitterness that Denis ever showed in the many conversations with me was over the way both the BBC and *Express* abruptly ended his work with them. He was convinced, although it is strenuously denied by my BBC contacts, that he was chopped from the commentary team because of his campaign to keep cricket links open with South Africa. What hurt him even more was the way he was dumped by the *Express* after forty years as their voice of cricket. He was convinced it was personal, but I got the other side of the story from the man charged with the job of removing him, former *Sunday Express* Sports Editor Peter Watson, who got off the Fleet Street treadmill to prepare himself for the seniors' golf tour.

Story of a sacking

PETER WATSON: "My editor at the time, Eve Pollard, had ordered massive economy cuts, and she did not consider Denis right for the modern paper that she had in mind. I took Denis out to lunch and told him as gently as I could that I was happy to keep employing him but that I could no longer allow him the luxury of a ghostwriter. He was enormously upset and took it that I had sacked him. It was one of the saddest days in all my years as a sports editor, because along with everybody else I was extremely fond of him. But he was well into his seventies and we had a drive on for a younger readership. I would have liked to discuss with Denis the possibility of doing a sports nostalgia column, but I never got the chance. He put me top of his unpopularity list, and we never spoke again apart from one abusive telephone call in which he gave me the full length of his tongue. If I could turn the clock back I would have organised a massive farewell and thank you lunch for one of the greatest sportsmen this country has ever produced. But Denis put up a barrier between us, and became very sour over a situation that was none of my doing. How do you tell a legend that he is a yesterday's man? I found it very difficult explaining to him that we needed a fresh new voice, and I knew he was very disappointed when we turned to David Gower. The name of Denis Compton in the *Sunday Express* meant a lot for many years, but by the dawn of the nineties I am afraid only fifty-somethings and the senior citizens truly appreciated what a giant he had been. I considered it a great privilege to have known him, and I was very sad that it fell to me to be the one who had to bring what was an inevitable end to his *Sunday Express* column."

Desperately hurt

DENIS COMPTON: "I felt desperately hurt by my treatment by the *Sunday Express*. As I understood it, they had a dynamic woman editor who was anti anybody who could

160

be classed as a veteran. Reg Hayter was furious. He said it was a disgrace the way they kicked me out after forty years without any warning. Reg wanted to fight my corner, but I told him not to bother. I have never been one to stir up trouble, and I was not going to start now. I had many great friends on the *Express*, and it was so sad the way it ended."

Denis would have been missed most of all by the team on the *Daily Express*. He was a regular visitor to our sportsroom during my days reporting football for the paper. He used to give a pretty poor performance at pretending he had come down to see what was happening in the football world when it was transparently obvious that what he really wanted to do was pick the brains of the Holy Trinity of racing who occupied the adjoining desks. Peter O'Sullevan, Clive Graham and Charles Benson were all close chums of Compo, and did their best to satisfy his thirst for winners.

Enthusiastic punter
PETER O'SULLEVAN: "Denis had a deep knowledge of racing after many years as an enthusiastic punter. It was a joy to talk racing with him, but I'm not sure he always took the right advice. Denis was an impulsive, instinctive gambler, just as he was an impulsive, instinctive batsman who did things off the cuff. He was a grand man to know."

Earning power
JOHNNY HAYNES, former England and Fulham captain and the first £100-a-week British footballer: "I joined the Bagenal Harvey Organisation in the trail of Denis, and have him to thank for raising the profile and earning power of sportsmen. As I remember, Godfrey Evans and then I followed him as 'Brylcreem Boys'. Denis was a charmer of a man who was really refreshing in his approach to sport. He never treated it like life and death, and managed to give the impression he was playing for fun. When I was a youngster growing up

in London nearly every boy wanted to be Denis Compton. I should not think there has ever been a more popular sportsman."

I was among thousands of boys who followed the Compton lead and rubbed Brylcreem into my hair every morning in the hope that it would make me look and play like the great man [I would have needed to rub Aladdin's lamp for that].

There were ripples of laughter around Westminster Abbey when J.J. [John] Warr confided during his riveting address: "I changed alongside Denis in the Middlesex dressing-room on many occasions and can never once remember a Brylcreem jar anywhere within Compo's reach." I did not hear any laughter coming from the direction of Compo's many old advertising friends in the congregation.

It was easy to imagine the "Brylcreem Boy" smiling cheekily down on us.

16: A Marrying Man

*Denis always made female hearts flutter, yet
he is what I would call a real man's man.*
Eamonn Andrews

WHEN Eamonn Andrews presented Denis with the Big Red
Book at the end of his *This Is Your Life* tribute, Compo was
close to tears. He was surrounded by family and friends,
including his third wife Christine, Brian, his son from his
first marriage, sons Patrick and Richard from his second
marriage, daughters Charlotte and Victoria from his eleven
year marriage to Christine, along with five grandchildren who
had all been flown in from South Africa where his sons all
lived. Also filling the set with their love and respect for
Compo were his old Arsenal skipper Joe Mercer, along with
former cricketing colleagues Keith Miller, Godfrey Evans,
Peter May, Alec Bedser, Trevor Bailey, Fred Trueman, Ted
Dexter, John Warr, Don Wilson, Alan Oakman, Fred Rumsey,
Colin Milburn, Colin Ingleby-Mackenzie, Doug Insole and ex-
England rugby wing hero Ted Woodward. Denis gave an
emotional, impromptu speech to the studio audience ...

A wonderful life
DENIS COMPTON: "I have been lucky to have had many
great days in my full life, but this beats them all. What more

can a man ask than to be surrounded by the people he cares about most of all? To have my children and grandchildren all together for the first time is as marvellous a gift as I could receive, and to see so many of my old sporting pals brings it home to me just what a wonderful life I have had. I have known Eamonn for many years, and congratulate him on catching me out. I honestly had no idea that this was going to happen, and there are not words to express how happy I feel. Thank you."

Eamonn Andrews was secretly battling against failing health, and none of us knew that this would be one of his final *This Is Your Life* assignments. He died later that year to bring to an end one of the great broadcasting careers that had its foundation in the world of sport.

Booked at last

EAMONN ANDREWS: "I had been wanting to present the Book to Denis ever since I first launched the British version of *This Is Your Life* back in the 1950s. There was always something cropping up to stop it, such as his change of partners and the passing of people vital to the story. He and I have known each other well since the days when I used to present *Sports Report* on radio, and I often had the pleasure of interviewing him. What I like so much about him is his humility. If anybody has cause to swagger it is Denis, whose sporting achievements were just phenomenal. But he has always been modest and self-effacing, and when you try to talk to him about his sporting triumphs he will volunteer facts about the times when his career was not going that well. He is as happy to talk about his ducks and the missed goals as he is about the moments that brought joy and excitement into the lives of thousands lucky enough to have seen him in his prime. I have known many sportsmen in my time. Denis, is without any question, one of my favourites. I am delighted to have been able to book him at last! I know

Christine will not mind me saying that we will get a lot of ladies switching on when they know that it is Compo's life that we are featuring. He has always made female hearts flutter, yet he is what I would call a real man's man."

Denis was a pin-up boy throughout his career and it was no secret that he liked the company of pretty ladies. He admitted to me that while on tours he used to receive a lot of invitations to visit the hotel rooms of beautiful women, but not being the boastful or indiscreet type he declined to say how many – if any – he accepted. His relationships rarely came under the scrutiny of the media in a climate far removed from today's when incessant invasion of privacy is the norm.

Lipstick invitation

DENIS COMPTON: "The temptations were always there. I remember once sitting having my dinner on board ship on the way to Australia when a beautiful blonde lady came from her table and asked me to autograph her menu. As she thanked me, she pushed her table napkin furtively into my hands. Written in lipstick on the napkin was the number of her cabin. Even now as I gallop towards old age I get elderly women coming up to me and telling me that they adored me during my cricketing days. It's nice to hear because I have always liked to look at the ladies. You can have a work of art at home, but that doesn't mean you cannot appreciate other masterpieces! I think it fair to say that I was always one of the boys."

Compo's first marriage to a beautiful dancer called Doris followed a wartime romance that had cooled by the early post-war years. The union produced a son, Brian, who often pops up in old black and white newsreels being shown how to bat by his father. It is surprising in how many of those old film clips and photographs you see Denis with a lighted cigarette in his hand, although he always assured me that he was just a puffer and never a serious smoker.

He met his second wife Valerie, who was from a wealthy South African family, during the England Springbok tour of 1948-9. It was the English climate as much as anything else that torpedoed the marriage. Valerie wanted to bring up their two sons with the sunshine of South Africa on their backs. Denis would have been happy living in what he often called his 'second country' but his English roots were too deep, and he sadly agreed to a divorce.

His marriage to Christine, who had been a dynamo of a PA in Bagenal Harvey's office, followed in 1972 just as fifty-four-year-old Denis seemed resigned to a bachelor's life. The two daughters that Christine gave him, Charlotte and Victoria, who arrived when he was sixty-six, put a new spring in Compo's step even though hip problems had taken over from The Knee as his most painful handicap.

It was sad to see the usually even tempered Compo become quite crotchety and short tempered when ill health started to grip him in his later years, but this was understandable considering the pain he was often in. He was also having problems with diabetes, and he was eaten up with frustration at the fact that he could not get around without the aid of a stick. It was Christine and the daughters – "my three girls", Compo called them – who helped ease what had become a difficult passage into senior citizenship. After his *This Is Your Life* tribute, he went out of his way to acknowledge to me the importance of Christine in his life.

A very lucky man

DENIS COMPTON: "Christine is the best thing that ever happened to me, and I worship her. She not only gives me the love and attention that I need, but is so superbly organised that she helps me keep my life in some sort of order. I am not the easiest person to live with because the problems I am having with my hips make me quite moody at times. But Christine is like a rock for me, and the two daughters she has given me are very precious to us. They keep me young in mind. My first two marriages did not really have a chance to survive. Test cricketers have the hardest job of all to hold their marriages together because of all the touring. It went wrong with Valerie mainly because she did not like the English climate, and she also had to put up with my shifting moods caused by the agony I was in with my knee. I am very fortunate to have found Christine and to have her company and her love. I'm a very lucky man."

I passed on this compliment to Christine following Compo's memorial service at Westminster Abbey, and she revealed her well-tuned humour by telling me, "I think you are letting your scriptwriter's imagination run away with you!" But he *did* say it, Christine, and he did mean it. There was always bubbling fun between Christine and Denis, and we both teased him over the fact that I had briefly been her 'husband' when sitting in for him during the rehearsals for his *This Is Your Life* programme. It was a night when the years fell away from Denis as he revelled in being the focal point of a huge family reunion.

Of his three sons, only Brian from his first marriage [who became a personnel director in Johannesburg] could recall seeing him play. His father bought him a bat and gave him coaching lessons, but despite this early encouragement he was never able to follow in his dad's footsteps. Patrick and Richard, his sons from his marriage to Valerie, both established themselves as journalists in Durban. Neither inherited their dad's special sporting gifts, but both are immensely proud of all that he achieved and the *This Is Your Life* programme underlined for them his special standing in the sports world.

Who's the greatest?

BRIAN COMPTON: "During the 1948 Test series against the Australians at the Oval, Dad took me along to watch the game. I think that it was in one of the lunch intervals that Keith Miller showed me around the Australian dressing-room and introduced me to the one and only Don Bradman. 'This is Don Bradman,' said Keith. 'Now, who's the greatest batsman in the world?' Both Don and Keith laughed out loud when I said, 'My dad, of course.' It is well-known history that this was the Test in which The Don played his last innings and got a duck when just four runs short of a perfect average of one hundred. Perhaps I had unsettled him! I can remember Dad giving me lessons in how to bat, but is there anybody who could have followed in his footsteps? Dad was a one-off."

Sir Gubby Allen had planned to join the *This Is Your Life* show but became unwell, and his contribution was confined to a live telephone call in which he told the story of the umpire giving Denis out in his debut because he wanted to spend a penny (see page 35). Had he been able to come on, he was going to apologise to Denis for possibly costing him five England Test caps.

An apology from Gubby

SIR GUBBY ALLEN: "I had the casting vote as England skipper when we were discussing whether to take eighteen-year-old Denis on the 1936-7 Ashes tour to Australia. It was my view that he was too inexperienced, and I was concerned that a bad tour could wreck his confidence and spoil one of the greatest prospects we had ever produced. In subsequent years as I watched Denis develop and got to know him as a good friend I realised that I had been wrong with my assessment. He had the sort of approach that meant he would have flourished Down Under. The bigger the occasion the better he played. Denis represented England seventy-eight times in his distinguished career. I am very sorry that it was not eighty-three Tests, and I want to offer my profound apologies to Denis."

The after-show party at the Teddington Lock studios in the Compton territory of Middlesex went on to the early hours, with Denis one of the last to leave. He made the point of going to every person who had appeared on the programme to thank them for coming; and he also found time to tell the *This Is Your Life* production team how much he appreciated their efforts in putting the show together. It was a typical well-mannered, thoughtful act by a thoroughly nice man.

Denis also playfully pummelled Nick Owen and myself for the part we had played in the pre-show subterfuge. "I'll never trust you again," he told me. "All those talks we've had, and I thought it was all because you were a fan of mine!" With the conspiratorial blessing of Christine, Nick Owen – then an ITV sports presenter – and I had drawn Denis to the Teddington studios under the pretence that Thames Sport were producing a programme on great sporting heroes. We kept the charade going as Denis was being prepared in the make-up room for his appearance in front of the television cameras. We all roared when the girl applying the make up asked Denis, "Can I have your autograph, Mr. Compton?" Compo was just removing a pen from his pocket, when she added: "It's for my grandma. She used to have a picture of you on her bedroom wall."

To keep Compo convinced that he was about to appear on an interview show about great heroes, Nick had a notepad page full of questions that he put to Denis to get him primed for what he was convinced was a programme looking back on his career. It was a session that helped me get extra background facts for this book. At the after-show party, with Denis acting as an enthusiastic orchestrator, the night was brightened by a procession of Compo stories ...

On the nose
TED WOODWARD, former England rugby wing-threequarter hero: "Denis and I are regular golfing partners, and also follow the horses together. I was round his house recently

discussing the day's racing, and told Denis that I had a strong tip that Wayward Lad was a good thing at ten-to-one for the Cheltenham Gold Cup. He signalled with his eyes for me to follow him out of earshot of the lovely Christine. I went into the kitchen with him and he slipped me thirty pounds. 'It's out of the housekeeping,' he said. 'Not a word to Christine. Put it on the nose.' That afternoon I watched the race with him on television, and he did not blink an eyelid as Jonjo O'Neill brought the favourite Dawn Run through with a late run to pip Wayward Lad for first place. 'Oh well,' he said. 'There's only one thing for it. Let's have another bottle of bubbly.' I think that about sums up his zestful approach to life. He does love a bet, whether it's on the golf course or the racecourse. Win or lose, his mood is never affected."

Autograph hunter

TED DEXTER: "I idolised Denis when I was a lad, and joined a queue of jostling schoolboys for his autograph during his golden summer of 1947 when I was twelve and at my most impressionable. Denis was renowned for never refusing an autograph, but he was preoccupied on this particular day during the Test match against the South Africans at Lord's and he apologetically rejected my proffered piece of paper. I had never before and have never since asked anybody for an autograph! He had a fairly impressive match, putting on 370 in a record third-wicket partnership with Bill Edrich. The autograph snub did nothing to lessen my admiration for Denis and his wonderfully intuitive and exciting batting. Our careers just overlapped, and it is one of my proud boasts that I twice took his wicket in what was one of the last Gentlemen versus Players matches. But I hastily have to confess that this was not the Compton who had terrorised and tamed attacks throughout his marvellous career. Many years later, when he was into his mid-fifties and suffering from gout, I saw him play in a charity match. He danced down the wicket to the first ball he received and hit it clean out of the ground. It was evidence, if evidence was needed, that he had perfect coordination of hand and eye. It was Denis who introduced me to my agent Bagenal Harvey, an association that worked very well for me. In return I think I should have bought Denis a watch. He never used to wear one, and was without doubt the worst timekeeper I have ever known. I prided myself on being a better racing tipster than Denis, and we used to have competitions as to who could select most winners. He has been a winner all his life."

A caring man
COLIN MILBURN, who lost an eye in a car crash in 1969 just a few weeks after scoring a Test hundred against the West Indies: "One of the first cheer-up notes I received was from my hero, Denis. He kept taking time out to encourage me and telling me how Tiger Pataudi had played Test cricket with one eye. We have had many a good drink together, and I have a hazy recollection of him once pouring me into a car and making sure I was delivered back to my hotel. As well as being one of our greatest ever batsmen he is also a very caring man, and like everybody else in cricket I think that his knighthood is long overdue."

The forgotten box
GODFREY EVANS: "Everybody has stories to tell about Denis being forgetful. I have seen him arrive at the last minute before the start of a day's play and dash out to the wicket wearing borrowed boots and kit and carrying the first bat that he picked up on his way out of the dressing-room. A hundred or so runs later he would return as if it was an everyday event. The funniest thing I saw was when he was going out to bat against Miller and Lindwall at their fastest during the 1948 series. He had gone down the steps to a tumultuous cheer from his army of fans, and then suddenly turned and ran back to the pavilion. As he scrambled through his cricket bag he told us, 'I've forgotten my box.' Denis and

I used to share a bat when playing for England, a lovely lightweight thing that weighed just two pounds two ounces. It was a magic wand in his hands, and more like a cudgel in mine. Denis had borrowed it from his old Middlesex team-mate Jack Young. It was crafted by the Middlesex batmaker Harry Warsop, but because Denis had a contract to play exclusively with a Wisden bat Harry replaced his logo with that of Wisden. But I can tell you that all Compo's runs in 1947 were made with a Warsop!"

An early bath
JOE MERCER: "Both Denis and Leslie were lovely lads, who helped the great team spirit we had at Arsenal. I remember once our enormously strong manager Tom Whittaker playfully picking them both up and throwing them fully dressed into the team bath after they had taken the mickey out of him. Denis would have had a cupboardful of England caps but for the war, but there was not a trace of jealously when big brother Leslie got his first England cap. He was as thrilled as if it had been awarded to him, and sent him a telegram from Australia where he was on tour saying, 'Well done, Big Head.' That was the affectionate nickname for Leslie, who had a similar temperament to Denis and could be relied on in any crisis. I've hardly been out of my home recently because I have not been feeling too well. Denis is the one man for whom I would put myself out to pay my respects. He has been one of the greatest sporting ambassadors we have ever had, and I consider it a pleasure and a privilege not only to have known him but to have played on the same patch of grass."

Spectacular run out
SIR ALEC BEDSER: "I was the victim of one of Denis's most spectacular run out mix-ups. He had bravely returned to the wicket in the 1948 Old Trafford Test against Australia after having his forehead gashed when he mishooked a Lindwall

bouncer. I was at the other end hoping to be able to keep my wicket intact while Denis collected the runs in that dashing style of his. Denis decided to go for a run, then changed his mind. I was careering back to the crease when Don Bradman and Sam Loxton collided trying to field the ball. 'Right then,' shouted Denis, 'let's go for it.' I turned too quickly, got myself in a tangle and watched helpless as my bails were removed while Bradman and Loxton looked on from their positions on the floor. What a pantomime. It should have been a comfortable run, but there was no such thing in Denis's book! He went on to score 145 despite his sore head, so how could I complain? The following year in South Africa I was at the wicket batting with Cliff Gladwin when we ran a leg bye off the last ball of the match to win by two wickets. When I asked Denis what he thought of my performance, a magnificent one not out, he said, 'Sorry, Alec. I couldn't bear to watch and locked myself in the lavatory!' That was the game in which he scored a brilliant 72 on a pig of a pitch and bowled 11 maidens in 16 overs. It is often forgotten that Denis was a good quality left-arm spinner, who could have been a match–winning bowler had he been able to give more time to perfecting his flight and spin."

Bar-room buzz

J.J. (JOHN) WARR: "Denis has brightened many a day for me, not only on the field of play but into his senior citizenship. We are near neighbours and often meet in our local bar at the Belgium Arms for what we call a 'snifter and nostalgia' session. He is a kind, generous and warm man, and even now that he is handicapped by troublesome hip problems he still carries on in cavalier spirit. When he walks into the bar there is always a buzz around the place as those who know the great sportsman that he was whisper to younger companions about his feats that had to be seen to be believed. I have never known anybody so disorganised and untidy in a dressing-room, and invariably you would lose an item of clothing or cricket equipment, only to find that Denis had packed it by mistake. But nobody could take umbrage against Denis. He would give you that rascal smile of his, and all was quickly forgiven. I was delighted that Eamonn Andrews trapped him with the Book. Nobody has better deserved to have his life story told than Denis, and I hope that the younger generation watching will now fully appreciate what a genius he was. And yes, I do mean genius. Eamonn asked me what I planned as a contribution to the programme. I told him that I was going to come on and greet Denis with the words, 'I really enjoy your performances, Compo, in *Last of the Summer Wine*.' Eamonn tried not to look too horrified and quickly reduced me to just a walk-on part. Had I been allowed to speak, I would have told the nation that Denis was one of the finest sportsmen we have ever produced. I cannot think of any one person who has given so much pleasure to so many people. He always played the game and lived his life in the right spirit."

Bad timekeeper

TREVOR BAILEY: "There is only one person I know who is as untidy and as bad a timekeeper as Denis - and that's me! I'm the man who once missed the boat-train at the start of a South African tour. In one of the more curious combinations that I can ever remember, Denis and I were paired together as hotel room-mates on the rather eventful 1953-4 tour of the West Indies. It is a toss up as to which of us suffered the more, but I recall that Denis acquired as many garments marked 'T.E. Bailey' as I did those marked 'D.C.S. Compton.' We used to call him 'Golden' because of his luck with the horses and at the card table. But he was very generous with his winnings, and I had many excellent meals on Denis after he had cleared the pot at the card table or walked away from the racecourse with a pocketful of winnings. I was on the receiving end of one of his infamous run negotiations in the 1954 Old Trafford Test against Pakistan. He hit the ball and shouted, 'Right.' I was backing up and quickened my pace, until suddenly Denis changed the call to 'Wait!' His next shout was a very definite 'No!' By this time I was in no man's land as I slammed on the brakes and did a three-point turn before trying to regain my ground. I was a yard short, and as I made the long, lonely walk back to the pavilion I dwelt on the thought that I had been a victim of Denis's three-call trick! He averaged over ninety in that series and this when he was severely handicapped by his knee problem. Goodness knows what his Test output would have been but for the war and then The Knee."

Throwing the bottle

FRED TRUEMAN: "There was the infamous bottle-throwing riot on that West Indies trip that Trevor was talking about. I remember Denis casually lobbing one of the bottles back into the crowd after pretending to drain it. I told him that if I'd done that I would have been sent back home on the next banana boat. 'Yes, Fred,' he said, 'but I used a slow left-arm delivery. You'd have bounced it back into the crowd!' Denis was a great cricketer and a great companion."

Postcard reminders

DOUG INSOLE: "We all know about Denis being, what shall I say, fairly unreliable. I once asked him to play in a charity match for me, and to make sure he did not forget I sent him a postcard every week leading up to the match. Dear old Denis turned up as good as gold. He shrugged and smiled when he was informed that he was expected at two other matches on that same day! My assessment of Denis is that he was an absolutely brilliant batsman and a top-class footballer, but, above all that, he is a bloody good bloke."

Wrong birthday

COLIN INGLEBY-MACKENZIE, President of the MCC and former captain of Hampshire: "The TV cameras were showing a live tribute to Denis at London's Café Royal on what was reported to be the grand occasion of his fiftieth birthday. Speaker after speaker rose in praise of the great man reaching his half-century. Suddenly the red-coated master of ceremonies escorted Denis to a telephone where an urgent call was waiting. It was his mother telling him, 'Denis, you are a naughty boy. You are only forty-nine!' I cannot swear to this story being true, but – knowing Denis – it probably is. I cannot think of anybody who has had a greater influence on an entire generation of cricketers than Denis. He inspired all of us to get hold of a bat and try to become Denis Compton. But, of course, he was quite unique and it was impossible to make a copy. When I was captain of Hampshire I got a lot of publicity with my little joke, 'I always insist on my players being in bed by nine-thirty ... after all the match starts at eleven.' Denis telephoned to congratulate me. That really appealed to his entertainment-first philosophy on cricket and life. I am proud to call him a dear friend, even though he is one of the worst horse racing tipsters in captivity!"

The last catch
KEITH MILLER: "What I have kept from everybody in case you cancelled my trip is that Denis and I were last together just a short while ago. He was a fly-in guest on *my This Is Your Life* in Australia! You could not tell either of our life stories without including each other. We have an unbreakable bond that goes back to the springtime of our lives. In my farewell match in England during the 1956 end-of-season Scarborough Festival I hoiked a shot to long off and there was Compo galloping on that gammy knee of his to take a great catch. The crowd roared, and then wondered what was going on when Denis dropped the ball and signalled 'no catch'. It was a gesture that captures his sportsmanship. I was not having any of it, and walked. Denis and I went off with our arms round each other at the end of the match as

the band played 'Auld Lang Syne'. It was the last time we played against each other apart from in charity matches. There may have been tears mixed with our champagne that night. What a way to finish. I could think of nobody better to have with me on the pitch than dear old Compo."

Champagne glass in hand, Denis listened to all the stories being swapped about his life and times, and positively glowed with pleasure. He added bits and pieces here and there like a master chef seasoning his own exclusive dish, and there were some stories that he dismissed as "made up by the fairies, old boy". He had us roaring when he said that if half the tales about his playboy adventures were true he would by now be an exhibit in the jar of a research unit. "How many times," he was asked, "did you turn up for a day's play wearing a dinner suit?" "Just once or twice," he said, pausing before adding with perfect timing, "... a season."

Getting shirty

DENIS COMPTON: "So much has come flooding back to me with all these memories that we have been sharing tonight. Trevor's story about me picking up his clothes reminds me of when I was fielding on the boundary in the 1946-7 Sydney Test. I always made a point of striking up conversations with spectators, and we were having a good old chin wag between overs, with me leaning back against the fence, when they started to fall about laughing and pointing at me. 'Can't you afford your own gear, Compo?' one of them shouted. I passed W.J. on my way to my next fielding place and said, 'Can you see anything about me that is making that lot laugh?' Bill gave me a close inspection and then started to laugh as well. 'I think you're better off discussing it with Jack Ikin,' he said. 'You've got his shirt on.' Somehow I had picked up one of Jack's shirts and had managed to put it on so that the label in the back of the collar was sticking up. It read, J.T. Ikin.

Another thing I recall from Trevor and Fred mentioning the West Indies tour is of being invited aboard Errol Flynn's yacht for a very lively party. But I'll tell you this, there has been no party for me to equal the one here this evening. Seeing so many of my dear old friends together again has given me the thrill of a lifetime. As Eamonn was listing all the things that I had managed to do, it made me realise what a lucky person I had been and also how quickly it had all gone. It's wonderful to have an occasion like this just to prove you were not dreaming it all."

Eamonn Andrews posed for one more picture with Denis for *This Is Your Life* stills photographer Stan Allan. It is a sequence of photos taken from the moment of the 'hit' at the top of the show that fill the final edition of the Big Red Book, which is given to the subject a week or so after the programme as a memento of their special night. Eamonn triggered another memory for Compo.

Radio times
EAMONN ANDREWS: "The first time I had a photograph taken with you, Denis, was in the BBC *Sports Report* studio in the days of steam wireless. It was December 1952 and I was interviewing you and Sir Jack Hobbs on the occasion of The Master's seventieth birthday [see the pictures section]. I remember clearly Sir Jack saying that you were the most exciting batsman he had ever seen. You responded by telling our listeners that Sir Jack had been your boyhood hero and that he was the finest English batsman of all time. You reached out to shake his hand at the end of the interview and managed to knock a glass of water all over my script! Now, in a twinkling of an eye, here we are not too far away from *your* seventieth year."

It was Compo who added, "Doesn't time fly when you're having fun. And it really has been great fun, you know."

17: Tales of the Unexpected

*I have no hesitation in describing Denis as the
most entertaining batsman I ever played with.*
Tom Graveney

DENIS COMPTON generated more stories in his life time than almost any other sportsman, many of them apocryphal and exaggerated but just as many amazingly true. I have tried to dig out the most entertaining of the tales of the unexpected, and kick off with three from the best of all the Compo storytellers, former Middlesex and England batsman Peter Parfitt. His brilliant after-dinner speeches are peppered with Compoisms.

The borrowed bat

PETER PARFITT: "Denis was kindness and generosity personified but quite autocratic in the changing-room where he was the senior pro by the time I started my career with Middlesex in the mid-1950s. He was so good that he didn't mind whose equipment he used. Anything lying loose in the dressing-room was fair game for him. I was sitting padded up on the balcony once during one of my early County matches anxiously watching the master at work at the wicket. I had my gloves by my side and was wound up

179

ready for action. Oh, how I flapped when I suddenly realised that he was out in the middle with *my* bat.

"In 1956 I was new to the Middlesex dressing-room. Although I played the first fourteen matches I was then left out and became twelfth man. The main duties consisted of going out on to the pitch to take messages from either Compo or the skipper Bill Edrich. Usually, this consisted of taking down their bet for the 3.30 at Goodwood and then making sure that it was placed. All this, of course, was before the dawn of betting shops and you had to deal on the old hush-hush with a bookie's runner. The trouble with the system was that if you were successful at it you could then expect to be twelfth man all year because both were superstitious to the point where they were convinced the messenger could have that lucky touch! But if their fancies lost, you had to brace yourself for some black looks – and a recall to the first team.

"On a sunny July afternoon in 1955 Denis walked into the Bull at Gerrards Cross for a refresher. They were delighted to see him but somebody wondered if Denis wasn't playing in the Test match due to start the following day at Old Trafford. The penny suddenly dropped with Denis. He was indeed supposed to have been in Manchester, and not only that, but he was due at net practice that very afternoon. He drained his glass and left in haste, persuaded a pal to fly him up north in his private plane and eventually arrived at Manchester in the early evening, too late for nets, but in time for dinner. He had finished the journey by train from Derby after the plane had been forced down by poor weather. Having left in such a rush he had no equipment and went out with borrowed kit, including the bat. He made 158."

Magical innings

FRED TITMUS: "It was my bat that Denis borrowed against the South Africans at Old Trafford. It was brand new and had cost me the earth. He was out of the dressing-room door with it before I could protest. We had lost two wickets for twenty-odd, but Denis flourished the bat as if he held it in his hands every day and played a magical innings. I went out to join him with a borrowed bat and was sent straight back for a duck. Thanks, Denis! I idolised the man, first of all as a footballer with Arsenal. It was only the fact that he doubled at cricket that inspired me to take up the game. What I particularly liked about Denis was the way he encouraged young Middlesex cricketers. Right up until he died he was always enquiring after their progress."

Over the fence
R.W.V. (WALTER) ROBINS: "Lovely chap, lovely cricketer, and it was a pleasure to be his skipper. But he was the worst timekeeper I have ever known. I deliberately used to give him starting times half an hour earlier than they really were in the belief that he might then at least make it in time for the first ball. During a County match against Sussex at Hove he overslept and arrived just as I was leading the players out for the start of play. He leapt over the boundary fence and took his place in the field, still wearing what looked like tennis shoes. I immediately tossed him the ball and told him to bowl, just to teach him a lesson. Goodness me, if he didn't take two wickets in his first two overs!"

In a spin
P.G.H. (PERCY) FENDER: "First time I clapped my eyes on young Denis was in the nets at Lord's. It was the summer of '34. I asked the coach Archie Fowler if he could spare a groundstaff boy while I turned my arm over, and he sent in this rather shy sixteen-year-old lad. I knocked his bails off with two googlies, one after the other. When I tried it a third time, he sent the ball scorching past me. He batted against me for about half an hour, and at the end of the session I told Archie, 'This lad is going to be a great asset to Middlesex, you mark my words.' More than forty years later I was with

Denis again, flying down to Melbourne for the Centenary Test. He reminded me of the two googlies, and he was kind enough to say that our session in the nets had helped him become such a great reader of spin. There was no better player of spin bowling."

Crafty tricks
EDDIE PAYNTER: "I was at the other end the day Denis scored his first Test century. That great character Bill 'Tiger' O'Reilly did everything he could to break Compo's concentration. 'My heavens, the pitch is taking more turn by the minute,' he shouted to wicket-keeper Ben Barnett for Compo's hearing. As Denis started to pick him off and collect runs, Tiger stood with his hands on his hips and looked down the wicket. 'Have mercy on a poor old Irishman,' he said. 'Let me have just one more wicket before I hang up my old boots.' Compo smiled back at the giant O'Reilly, but was not going to fall for his crafty tricks. When he reached ninety-eight, he came to me between overs and said, 'On your toes, Eddie. I don't want to hang about on the nervous nineties.' Fleetwood-Smith tried to confuse him with a looping ball, but Denis smacked it away and I ran like the wind to make sure he got his two runs. That lovely man O'Reilly shouted out, 'Well done, young Compo. This will be the first of many ... but not while I'm bowling, please!' Denis had this way about him that made him as popular with his opponents as he was with his team-mates."

Perfumed letters
JACK YOUNG, who was on the Lord's groundstaff with Compo and played alongside him through his Middlesex career: "We all used to be envious of Denis's mail. He was always getting young ladies sending him perfumed letters enclosing pictures of themselves and locks of hair. I wondered how he used to reply to them, but then after one match he gave me a lift in his car and I realised that he didn't

bother. The back seat was full of unopened letters. 'What are you going to do about all these?' I said. Denis shrugged. 'I just don't have time to answer them all, so I've decided the best thing is not to answer any of them.' He was the most disorganised person I had ever met, yet at the wicket he was always in complete control ... except when it came to taking a quick run. We played a match at Leicestershire once when he dropped his bat after calling for a sharp single and nearly tripped me up as he bent down to pick it up. Life was always entertaining when Denis was at the wicket."

Pitch invasion

LINDSAY HASSETT, former Australian skipper: "I met up with Denis in India near the end of the war. I was skippering an Australian Services team, and we agreed to play the East Zone of India on our way back from playing some charity fund-raising matches in England. We thought we were going to meet a team of Indians, so you can imagine our surprise when they produced Denis as a guest player. He was burned nearly black by the sun, and I told him, 'It's no good trying to disguise yourself, Compo. We know who you are.' I had played against him in the 1938 Test series in England, and knew that the Indians had selected a real match winner. I top-scored with 125, and we looked in a strong position when Denis came in to bat after the East Zone had lost two quick wickets. He had just taken his guard when there was uproar on the terraces. A mob of rioters protesting against British rule rushed on to the pitch. As Keith Miller will tell you, the leader of the mob dashed up to Compo and said, 'You very nice man, Mr Compton, but you must go.' Denis, who had his bat raised like a sword, looked at me and said, 'What's your advice, Lindsay?' 'Well I don't know about you, Compo,' I said, 'but I'm off to the dressing-room for a nice cool beer.' We then raced off as fast as our legs would carry us. Keith had us in fits when he told Compo, 'There's only one Pom in the ground and you start a bloody riot!'"

Betting bug

GODFREY EVANS: "It was a toss up whether Denis or I had the biggest betting bug. I bet it was me! When we came together in the second innings of the fourth Test in Adelaide there were only a handful of runs needed to regain the Ashes. As I joined him at the wicket, Denis bet me a fiver that he would hit the winning runs. That might explain why he does not look overjoyed in the newsreels as I am seen nicking the winning run. Our good mate Keith Miller was the bowler, and he knew all about our bet. He was having a chuckle at Compo's expense as we came off. Magical days."

Bland memories

COLIN BLAND, who became a legendary fielder with South Africa: "It is one of my abiding memories that as a seventeen-year-old schoolboy I was sent out as a substitute fielder for my native Rhodesia against the MCC tourists at Bulawayo in 1956. Denis was approaching the last lap of his career on his bad knee, but he treated everybody to a magnificent knock of forty-nine before Percy Mansell clearly got him leg before. The umpire, obviously enjoying the innings as much as the rest of us, gave him not out. Denis being Denis could only play in the spirit of the game, and he deliberately spooned the next ball back into Percy's hands. The crowd gave him a standing ovation, as much for his sportsmanship as the sheer brilliance of his stroke play."

Sunburned tongues

MAURICE TREMLETT, former Somerset and England all-rounder: "Somerset were one of the few teams to beat Middlesex in the summer of 1947 when Bill and Denis were thrashing attacks all over the place. I was extremely nervous because it was my County debut, and I was overjoyed to clean bowl Denis before he could get his eye in. Then, to make it even more memorable, I hit the winning runs to go with my eight wickets in the match. The Middlesex players applauded me off the pitch and Denis went out of his way to come into the dressing-room to congratulate me on my performance. I think that typified his sporting approach to the game. The following May Somerset played Middlesex at Lord's, and, boy, did Denis and Bill make me pay for the success I had against them in my debut! They put on the little matter of 424 for the third wicket. We were chasing the ball all over the hallowed ground on a blazing hot day, and had sunburned tongues by the time Middlesex declared. They made 209 runs in just seventy minutes after tea. This sounds an exaggeration, but I know it's true because many of the runs were scored off me. Denis was dancing down the wicket before I had even released the ball, and no matter what I bowled he turned it into a full toss. I have never seen run making like it."

Playing for kicks

CYRIL WASHBROOK, former Lancashire and England opening master: "Indian opener Vijay Merchant had been giving England's attack a bit of hammer in the final Test at the Oval in 1946 when he decided to test Denis's throwing arm with a quick single. What he forgot is that Denis was also an exceptional footballer, and he kicked the ball left-footed into the stumps to run him out. I told him that it was just the sort of shooting accuracy that Manchester United could do with, but Denis, of course, was Arsenal through and through. Denis and I made our debuts in the same Test against New Zealand in 1937, and I had the pleasure of watching his Test career develop from close quarters. My opening partner Len Hutton and I used to shake our heads at the way he would prepare for an innings. While Len and I would lock ourselves into a cocoon of concentration, he would either be dozing in the dressing-room or playing cards – often, when it was raining, against members of the opposing team. He seemed to be able to treat it all so casually and then go out and play with astonishing innovation as if he had been making studious preparations for the innings. He was a remarkable cricketer."

The Sobers view
SIR GARFIELD SOBERS: "The first time I ever lost my wicket in a Test was to Denis. He held a fine catch after I had edged a shot from Tony Lock at Sabina Park in 1954. I was only seventeen at the time, and I had heard enough about the exploits of Denis to know that he was a giant of the game with the bat. I was a specialist left-arm spin bowler in those days, and I developed my googly and 'chinaman' after watching him bowl on that 1953-4 tour. He was an underestimated bowler, and might have got many more wickets had England not been so dependent on his batting. Like me, Denis enjoyed his horse racing and did not make the mistake of taking his cricket too seriously."

Wrong ball
RACHEL HEYHOE-FLINT, former England cricket captain and exceptional batswoman: "I adored Denis. He was such a lovely character who always had time to pass the time of day. I recall when he once agreed to turn out in a men versus women charity match. It would have been one of his last appearances on a cricket field. Denis spent too much time in the hospitality tent, and when it came his turn to bat I think he may have been seeing two balls. Anyway, he chose the wrong one to hit, and the ball trickled past his bat and gently dislodged his bails. Denis laughed all the way back to the hospitality tent, saying, 'Would you believe it, bowled first ball by a woman!' He came to the wicket laughing, and left it laughing. That, I feel, is an appropriate way to remember him."

Investment goes wrong
BILL EDRICH: "Denis was not the shrewdest at looking after his money, and Middlesex decided to try to help him

safeguard his record benefit takings by investing a great lump of it in the infamous Ground Nuts scheme. It was a venture that went badly wrong for thousands of investors, including poor old Compo. But he just took it in his stride, shrugging it off as 'one of those things'. He said to me, 'I wish I'd had the good sense to have put it all on the favourite at Kempton. At least I'd have got a run for my money.'" ·

The groaning skipper

BRIAN STATHAM: "Of all the batsmen I have played with or against, Denis was one of the greatest to watch – provided you were not bowling to him! He was more capable of tearing an attack to shreds than almost any other batsman, and was so nimble on his feet that no spinners could feel safe bowling to him. I doubt if there has been a more difficult batsman to bowl to because he was so unpredictable. What impressed me was his ability to hit the ball on the up, a risky way to play on our wickets but he had few problems because he had such a good eye. In the 1954-5 Test at Adelaide England needed ninety-four to clinch victory and the Ashes. What looked an easy job suddenly took on a new challenge when Keith Miller dismissed Bill Edrich, captain Len Hutton and Colin Cowdrey in a devastating twenty-ball spell and then magnificently caught Peter May. Denis was just picking up his bat to walk out when our skipper, hands covering his face, was heard to groan in the corner of the dressing-room, 'The so-and-sos have done us again ... they've done us.' It was not quite the confidence booster a player likes to hear as he is just about to go out to bat. But Denis took it all in his jaunty stride, and saw us home to a five-wicket victory. He was very prominent in the celebrations that night which went on to the early hours. As ever, he was wonderful company."

Anyone for Denis?

RT. REV. DAVID SHEPPARD, Bishop of Liverpool and former England opening batsman and captain: "I have a vivid memory of Denis scoring a breathtaking 278 against Pakistan in the second Test at Trent Bridge in 1954. I was deputising as skipper because Len Hutton was unwell, and in his end-of-play summary Jim Swanton said on television how Compton had looked regularly to me on the balcony for instructions from his captain. The truth is that a television had been installed in the dressing-room so that we could watch the men's singles final at Wimbledon between Jaroslav Drobny and Ken Rosewall. Denis was keen to know what was going on because he had backed Rosewall, and the signals coming from the balcony were the set scores in the tennis and nothing whatsoever to do with the Test match!"

Behind the wheel
ALAN OAKMAN, former Sussex and England all-rounder: "One of my favourite Denis Compton stories is of when he was sitting in heavy traffic on the Thames Embankment driving himself to the Oval for the final day's play in a Test match against New Zealand. A taxi driver sitting alongside him at traffic lights shouted through his open window, 'Hey, Denis, aren't you supposed to be at the Oval ... they're about to start play.' Denis had forgotten that on the last day play started half an hour earlier.

The Don is dropped ... twice
JACK CRAPP, former Gloucester and England left-hand bat, exceptional slip fielder and respected umpire: "Whenever I see Denis I always raise my hands in a sign of apology. I'm the man who cost him the prized wicket of Don Bradman. He twice confused The Don with his 'chinaman' in one over at Leeds in 1948, and each time the greatest batsman of all time edged the ball to me at slip, and each time I put it down because I, too, had been confused by the deliveries! Denis just shrugged off the disappointment, while I am sure any other bowler would have wanted to strangle me. I was more

devastated about it than Denis. Bradman went on to score 173 not out, his last century in Test cricket. And Denis could have had him, if only ..."

In two minds
BILL EDRICH: "Denis was an underrated bowler, but he never had the best of luck against Bradman. In the second Test at Sydney on the 1946-7 tour he cracked Denis for four successive fours on his way to a majestic 234. When the fourth ball hit the boundary rope Denis looked up to the sky as much as to say, 'What have I done to deserve this?' As we passed at the end of the over, he whispered, 'I think I've got him in two minds ... he doesn't know whether to hit me for a four or a six!'"

Transfer news
TOMMY TRINDER, the cockney comedian who was chairman of Fulham and a cricket fanatic: "The England cricketers were good pals of mine, particularly Denis because of our football connection. I used to kid him that he should leave Arsenal and come and play for Fulham where he would at least have had a good laugh. I always made a point of giving a special Christmas party for the team when we used to meet up on Australian tours. Denis came to me during one of the parties and said, 'I'm surprised you're letting Ronnie Rooke come to Highbury, Tommy.' I nearly spilt my drink with shock. There was I on the Fulham board and I had no idea one of our best players was being transferred across London to Arsenal. It cost me nearly as much in cables finding out what was going on as we collected in a transfer fee. Denis had got the news even ahead of the London newspapers because he had just happened to be ringing his brother Leslie to wish him a merry Christmas as the transfer deal was being set up. Les had picked up the gossip in the dressing-room. I used to time my working trips to Australia to coincide with England tours. Denis was enormously popular out there. I once had him up

on stage at one of my shows in Sydney and he got a standing ovation. I got him, Len Hutton and Bill Edrich singing that old tongue-twisting song, 'Shoeshine Susie ... sitting in a shoe-shine shop ... all day long she shines and sits ... all day long she sits and shines ...' The place was in uproar by the time they'd finished singing it. I told the lads to stick to their cricket and leave the funny business to me."

Dropped catches

TOM GRAVENEY, Mr Elegance of England batting: "I have no hesitation in describing Denis as the most entertaining batsman I ever played with. His sole object was to enjoy the game, and he transmitted this attitude to all those around him and the spectators. One of the few times I saw him looking less than happy on a cricket field was when he twice dropped South African Eric Rowan off the bowling of Alec Bedser at Headingley in 1951. The Yorkshire crowd really gave him what-for because Rowan had already ground out two hundred runs. It was all so dull that I think Denis had allowed his mind to wander. The spectators were really cruel to him, and jeered every time he fielded a ball. The Hutton versus Compton debate was at its peak and the Yorkshire fans were making no secret of which player they supported. Denis's sense of humour came through when he said later, 'Oh well, at least I gave them something to shout about. It had been pretty boring up until then!' Cricket was never boring when Denis was around."

Broken spell

LES COMPTON: "There was a spell immediately after the war when Denis could hardly put bat to ball. He had a scoring sequence that went 10, 0, 7, 0, 8, 0 and 1. It was the worst trot I had ever known him have, and his confidence was at an all-time low when he got a first-ball duck against the Indians in the first Test at Lord's. For the first time in his career, he was not going out to the wicket in a carefree mood.

He was really beginning to worry that he would not be able to regain his pre-war touch. The turning point came in the next match for Middlesex against Warwickshire at Lord's. That master of spin Eric Hollies got him to edge his first ball, and it rolled back behind him and hit middle stump ... without dislodging the bails! Denis told me later that he was convinced it was a sign that his fortunes had changed. He put the next ball from Eric into the pavilion with a gigantic six hit, and went on to score 122. From then on he just did not seem to be able to stop scoring runs."

Dressed for dinner

NORMAN YARDLEY, former Yorkshire and England captain: "It was nothing unusual to find Denis turning up for a day's play wearing a dinner jacket after being at a party the night before. There was one occasion on the 1946-7 Ashes tour when he arrived at a private party given by a mutual Melbourne friend wearing what was a familiar dinner jacket. The reason it was so familiar was that it was mine! I had hunted high and low for it, and finally went to the party in a lounge suit. Denis was full of his usual apologies, and explained that he had picked it out of the wardrobe in the room we were sharing thinking it was his. In actual fact he left his own dinner jacket behind in Sydney! But you could never take offence at Denis's forgetfulness. It was just another of his many endearing qualities."

Orphanage lessons

PAUL GIBB, former England and Essex wicket-keeper: "Denis was quite notorious for not keeping his appointments, and during the 1946-47 tour I got used to him not turning up for golf matches that we had arranged. There was one occasion when I felt particularly put out, and it was not until I picked up an Adelaide evening newspaper to find a photograph of the great man teaching cricket at an orphanage that I knew why he had failed to show. Denis went up a notch in my estimation that he had given up his golf to help those poor unfortunates."

Twin trouble

ERIC BEDSER: "No matter how long Denis spent in our company, he could never tell for certain which was my twin brother Alec and which was me. He once came into the dressing-room after Alec had taken five wickets for the MCC in a brilliant spell and thumped me on the back, saying, 'Great bowling Alec.' Playing for Middlesex against Surrey in 1952, he hooked a bouncer from Peter Loader and got right over the ball and directed it down. It crashed towards close square leg where I was fielding and landed on the toecap of my boot. The ball ballooned and our wicket-keeper Arthur McIntyre made the catch standing well back. It was typical of Denis that he did not wait for the umpire to make a difficult decision, and walked. He looked over his shoulder, grinned at me and said, 'You lucky so-and-so, Alec!'

It ain't half hot mum

HARRY POTTS, Burnley inside-forward and later their manager: "I was in the All India Services Select football team that toured India and Burma in the last weeks of the war under the captaincy of Denis. His pre-match tactical talk in the dressing-room – or jungle clearing, as it often was – used to go something like this, 'Okay chaps, let's go out and enjoy ourselves. There's a pint waiting for the first player to score. Good luck.' There was one match against a team of bare-footed Indian players when we were running up a cricket score, and it was so one-sided that at half-time Denis instructed, 'We are embarrassing them, and that's not what we're here for. Hold off on the tackles and let them back into the game.' It was typical of Denis that he did not want to see anybody humiliated on the sportsfield. After every game, usually played in steaming-hot conditions, we would sign autographs for the servicemen, and it was nothing unusual for Denis to sit for more than an hour signing his name and chatting about cricket and football back home. There must be literally hundreds of soldiers who served in India who have Compo's autograph."

They shoot horses

JOE MERCER: "Our manager Tom Whittaker telephoned me at home a few days before Arsenal were due to play Burnley in the fifth round of the FA Cup in 1950. 'I'm thinking of picking Denis on the left wing,' he said. 'What d'you think?' 'Well,' I said, 'he's at least a stone overweight and his bellows are out of condition ... he's got a dodgy knee ... he's hardly played all season and is rusty ... and I should not think he's good for more than about sixty minutes. But I would pick him, too. That golden left foot of his just might turn the game for us.' Tom gambled, and Denis played a blinder. He made the first goal for Reg Lewis and scored the second himself with a cracking cross-shot. Whether it was cricket or football, he was a marvellous big-occasion player. He sat hunched in the dressing-room after the Burnley match, a cigarette in his hand and with steam rising from him. He had given everything. 'If I was a racehorse,' he said, 'I think you'd have to shoot me.' But he recovered to play a vital role in getting us to Wembley."

Picking up the bill

JIMMY GREAVES: "The last time I saw Denis was in the mid-nineties when he came to London Studios to take part in a *Sport In Question* show that I was fronting with Ian St John. He was on two sticks after a second hip replacement operation, and I had not been too long out of hospital myself after having a dodgy knee put right. 'We're picking up the bill for all that running around we did in the summertime of our lives,' I said to Compo. 'True,' he said, 'but I would not swap a second of it.' A youngster in the audience, who was about fifteen, came up and asked for Compo's autograph. 'I don't really know who you are,' he said, 'but my dad says that you were the greatest thing on two feet.' Denislaughed and said, 'Yes, my boy, but that was in another life.' I told the lad, 'When you show that signature to your mates tell them that it is the autograph of England's greatest sportsman.' I don't think too many people would argue with that assessment."

Wrong birthplace

DICKIE BIRD, legendary umpire and former Yorkshire and Leicestershire batsman: "I don't mind admitting that I cried my eyes out the day that Denis died. I admired him as a cricketer and loved him as a man. He became a very good friend of mine, and I used to joke with him that he made only one mistake in life. 'You should have chosen your birthplace better,' I used to tell him. 'You should have been born in God's county, Yorkshire'. Imagine if we'd had Len *and* Denis in our team together! We would have been unstoppable. Whenever Denis played in Yorkshire the crowd used to get on at him, usually about his Brylcreemed hair or about his football. But I'll tell you this, all Yorkshire folk admired and respected him as a cricketer. He always played the game in the right spirit, and he was loved wherever he waved that magic bat of his. You can bet your boots we won't see another like him."

A trip to Bendigo

PAUL GIBB: "Wally Hammond was one of the few people Compo could not melt with his charm. On the 1946-7 tour Hammond got up all our noses by travelling everywhere in a specially laid on Daimler while the rest of the team had to make do with buses and trains. As captain, he should have been with the troops. Denis felt in need of a rest after a hectic start to the tour, and he politely asked for a break. Hammond responded by leaving him out of the team to play in upstate Bendigo but insisted that he travelled the several hundred miles as twelfth man. Denis was not pleased because he had organised a little day out for himself at the races."

Out of bounds

ROY ULLYETT, the king of sports cartoonists and Compo's long-time colleague on *Express* Newspapers: "I was once playing in a charity golf tournament at Wentworth back in the 1950s with Denis, who was being partnered by Henry Cotton. Denis hooked the ball out of bounds off one tee, and jokingly claimed a six. He put down another ball and shanked it into the rough. Henry Cotton, one of our greatest ever golfers, watched all this with quiet amusement, and said, 'Now I know how your partners feel, Denis, when you run them out.' Denis had a good laugh at his own expense. He was a good sport, who always had a twinkle in his eye and was excellent company whether it was at a cricket match, on the golf course or in one of Fleet Street's watering holes."

A joy to watch

FRANK TYSON: "The most extraordinary innings that I saw Compo play came three years after he had officially retired. We were on a Cavaliers tour of South Africa in 1960, and Springbok off-spinner Hugh Tayfield was causing mayhem. Then Compo came to the crease on his suspect knee and proceeded to dispatch Tayfield to every point of the ground, working his way anticlockwise around the field as the South Africans tried to plug the holes. His knock lasted an hour and produced seventy of the most entertaining runs I had ever seen scored. It was an innings that epitomised Compton – a full-of-life gambler who thrived on taking chances and who was a joy to watch, unless you were the bowler on the receiving end."

Wearing a helmet

WAYNE LARKINS, England opening batsman in the 1980s: "Denis visited us in the Northants dressing-room once and

I asked him if he had ever tried on a helmet. 'You would never have got me to wear one of those things,' he said. 'I rarely even wore a cap.' We talked him into putting on a helmet and then got him to wear all the protective equipment that had been introduced since his playing days. He could not believe it. 'How d'you walk in all this stuff, let alone play in it?' he said. 'Imagine how many team-mates I would have run out weighed down by this!' We told him we were equally astonished he was able to face the likes of Lindwall and Miller without a helmet. Denis was even more flabbergasted when he tried our bats. He could not believe how heavy they were. I was never lucky enough to see him play, of course, but from everything you hear and from his record it is obvious that he would have been a great batsman in any era."

Missing school

TERRY LAWLESS, boxing manager and all-round sports enthusiast: "I played truant just once during my schooldays. It was in 1948 and I played hookey to go to Lord's to see the Middlesex–Somerset game. Compo, of course, was the magnet. He and Bill Edrich put on the little matter of 424 for the third wicket. It was unbelievable. Years later I told Denis that I had seen this innings, and asked him to talk me through it. 'Wish I could, old boy,' he said, 'but I was too busy scoring the runs to note how I was doing it!' He was as big a hero to me as my all-time favourite fighter, Sugar Ray Robinson. Both were unmatchable at their peak."

Journey into the unknown

TED WOODWARD, former England rugby star and Compo's long-time golfing partner: "There was an urgent telephone call for Denis at the end of the Saturday's play against South Africa in the 1947 Test at Old Trafford. He had just put his feet up in the dressing-room after finishing not out on sixty something, and was looking forward to a relaxing drink and a Sunday off with friends in Lancashire. On the telephone, the snooty secretary of Denham Golf Club said that he should lunch at the club tomorrow because there was important news for him. 'It was more of an order than a request, and he insisted it was not the sort of thing that could be conveyed on the telephone,' said Denis. So he got into the little Morris that he was driving then and motored the five hours in those pre-motorway days to Denham. The chairman of the committee announced at lunch that Denis had been accepted as a member of the club. And that was it. He then drove the five hours back and completed his century the next morning. Being the lovely, easy-going character that he was, Denis did not give the committee the rollicking they deserved for dragging him all the way from Manchester for news that could easily have waited a few days. But being a member at Denham has given Denis nearly as much pleasure as anything else in his wonderful sporting career, and the golf we have played together has never been anything less than fascinating. He has been a single handicapper who tends to play golf like he played cricket, with a lot of unpredictable shots. He is great fun on the golf course, and always likes a little sidebet to add some spice."

The last hole

REG GUTTERIDGE, ringside commentator known as the Voice of Boxing: "I played with Denis the day he decided he would reluctantly have to give up golf. He was playing on plastic hips and I was playing on one leg, having lost the other on the Normandy Beaches. He was into his seventies, and we were paired together in a charity match. We could not have even entered a three-legged race between us. I had known Denis from back in his Middlesex and Arsenal days, and had watched him play with my idol Alex James. We had shared Bagenal Harvey as an agent, and had a lot in common. Now here we were, two veterans hobbling to and from my golf buggy. As he sunk his final putt, Denis said, 'That's it. It's been great but the time has come to bow out.

I've loved every second of it.' And we loved every second of Denis, the Great Entertainer.

"I was introducing the guests at a National Association of Boys' Clubs dinner at the Café Royal in 1995. Denis had not been in good health, but he went along to support the charity dinner. I told Denis I was going to introduce him last of all after a procession of outstanding modern sports stars. 'But will they remember who I am?' Compo asked. He got the biggest round of applause of the night. There's only one Denis Compton."

When I was a football reporter on the *Daily Express* in 1966, I helped the legendary crime reporter Percy (later Sir Percy) Hoskins organise a Saints and Sinners lunch at which Bobby Moore was the guest of honour. Percy was the motivating force behind the charity fund-raising club, and as reward for helping him I was seated at the top table between England captain Moore and premier conductor Sir Malcolm Sargent. Sitting on Bobby's right was Denis Compton.

It was left to each guest to decide whether to wear a white carnation as a Saint, or a red one as a Sinner. Sir Malcolm and Compo chose white. Mooro and I elected to go for red, the colour of England's shirts when Bobby had lifted the World Cup for England just weeks earlier.

Bobby admitted that he was in awe of Compo. "You, more than anybody," he told the old warrior, "were the player I wanted to be when I was a boy. I was as much into cricket as football, and in fact the first time I ever played with Geoff Hurst was for Essex schools ... at cricket. I really envied you being able to combine both sports. By the time I became a professional, you had to choose between football and cricket. Which one would you have chosen?"

Denis had no hesitation in saying cricket, but he added, "I suppose financial considerations might have forced me to select football. I was so fortunate to have the best of both worlds. It would have been torture trying to decide which game to play. I just cannot imagine living my life without cricket. In fact it does not bear thinking about."

Sir Malcolm Sargent, darling of the Proms, told Bobby: "If I ever get the time, I would like to set the film of the 1966 World Cup final to music. It cries out for a concerto all of its own."

Sadly, Sir Malcolm died just a few months later without putting his idea to work.

I would like to see one of Compo's innings put to music: *The Compton Rhapsody.*

18: The Last Over

*Denis could mix comfortably with
kings and queens and the working
man. Everybody loved Compo.*
Keith Miller

WE finish this anecdotal celebration of the life and times of
Denis Compton where we started, at Westminster Abbey.
Apart perhaps from Lord's (Compo's second home), there
could not have been a more fitting venue at which to say
our final farewell to arguably the greatest English sporting
hero of all time.

The two thousand of us lucky to get tickets for Compo's
glorious last stand gathered at the Abbey on 1 July 1997,
fifty years exactly from the golden summer when he filled
the playing fields of England with more runs in a season
than any batsman has scored before or since. But it was
much more than his runs for Middlesex and England and
his goals for Arsenal and England that we were
remembering. We were remembering the man, a sporting
hero for all seasons.

There used to be a great Welsh boxer called Jimmy Wilde,
who was appropriately nicknamed the Ghost with a Hammer
in his Hand. Compo was the Artist with a Bat in his Hand,
who painted sunshine into so many lives.

The Abbey was filled with the spirit of Compton. It was a

suitably solemn occasion when necessary, but faces were continually wreathed in smiles as memories were conjured of his run making and his fun making. For Compo, sport was strictly for pleasure; and while he was enjoying himself he took us spectators along with him into the field of dreams that was his permanent place of residence. We all wanted to play like Compton, but we mere mortals had to make do with letting him live our fantasies for us.

Looking around the Abbey, it was as if someone had gathered the collection of cigarette cards from our schooldays and spread them out on to the historic flagstone floor. There were the Bedser twins, and over there Godfrey Evans, and Tom Graveney, as elegant as ever, and Ted Dexter with Colin, now Lord, Cowdrey. Reunited were old bowling rivals Brian Statham and Compo's soul mate Keith Miller; and beside them Dennis Amiss, with Fred Titmus, who took up cricket simply because his hero Denis Compton played the game.

Seeming somewhat bewildered by it all was one of today's heroes, Mark Ramprakash, the Middlesex captain who led his blazered County team-mates to the Abbey. It was almost as if he felt like a guest arriving too late for a party and wondering what he had missed.

How do you explain to him or any of his generation what they missed in not seeing Compton in full flow? Compo was one of the greatest party givers ever. He had us all drunk with the heady wine of his artistry. There have been greater batsmen, certainly more technically correct and many who were more efficient in accumulating runs. But few, if any, could match him for originality, sheer entertainment value and the ability to grasp the moment and turn it into something memorable and magical with a spurt of spontaneous strokes.

Ramprakash looked around at the great and the good and the "ordinary" folk who had come to join in the thanksgiving for the life of Denis Compton.

"He must have been something very special," said the Middlesex captain.

Oh yes, he was that all right.

You see, he was the summertime of our lives, and we will always be warmed by the inextinguishable glow of his memory.

I can think of no better way of closing this celebration of Compo than with these perfectly crafted words delivered at the Thanksgiving Service by the Very Reverend Dr Wesley Carr, Dean of Westminster:

"We have gathered here in Westminster Abbey to thank God for the life of Denis Compton. Our various ages bear testimony to the impact of his life on several generations. The distances that some have travelled affirm the affection in which he was held. Sporting colleagues and adversaries on both the cricket and football fields join those who could only observe his prowess with awe. All of us, whatever our age and wherever we have come from, players and spectators alike, acknowledge the skills that he was given and which he so flamboyantly employed. We celebrate the pleasure that he gave us and so many others. Whatever our faith, whether profound, tentative or none, we each thank God for a life enjoyed and lived to the full. We pray that Denis Compton's example may inspire for good all who recall his sporting career and especially those in coming generations who will try to copy his sportsmanship and skills."

God Bless, Compo. The light has gone out, but the memory will never dim.

EXTRAS

Compo's heroes,

The Scoreboard,

Chronology

The Storytellers

and

The Thanksgivers

Extras: Compo's heroes

Denis Compton was everybody's hero. He had an even better sweep shot than Dick Van Dyke in Mary Poppins
Eric Morecambe

COMEDIAN Eric Morecambe was a cricket lover who had three memorable terms as President of the Lord's Taverners, the charity organisation that performs wonders for the less fortunate in this world. I wrote a weekly "Sportslaugh" column in the *Daily Express* and *Titbits* in harness with Eric for six years, and it was his idea that I should compile a *Cricket Heroes* book, with a slice of the advance going to the Taverners. I had questionnaires completed by seventy of the top Test players. This was Compo's contribution.

MY CHILDHOOD BATTING HERO
The one and only **Sir Jack Hobbs**. My favourite treat when I was a lad was to be taken to Kennington Oval by my father to watch the great man in action. I used to study him through my father's field glasses and would marvel at his stroke play. He had a shot for every occasion. I was also a great admirer of his Surrey opening partner **Andrew Sandham**, who had to live in the shadow of The Master but was an excellent player in his own right with a full range of shots and a very sound defensive technique. I was also a devoted fan of **Patsy Hendren's** at Middlesex and had the privilege of playing with him in his final season. He was one of the greatest hookers of a ball I ever saw, and could really dominate an attack. Patsy kindly passed on many tips that helped make me a better batsman.

MY CHILDHOOD BOWLING HERO

Harold Larwood. Great pace was his prime weapon but he also kept an excellent line and length. I had the thrill of playing against Larwood and his partner Bill Voce in my second appearance for Middlesex. I hit the great man for three boundaries in his first over to me, but I have to admit that he was past his prime by then. He got me leg before in the second innings and I cannot recall receiving many faster balls throughout my career. The only English bowler I saw who could possibly match him for pace was Frank Tyson, who hit his peak on the 1954-5 tour to Australia.

MY IDEA OF THE PERFECT BATSMAN

Garfield Sobers and **Graeme Pollock**, both of whom were superb with the timing of their shots. Pollock had the gift of being equally strong on both front and back foot. Like all the great batsmen, his placing of shots was deadly accurate and he could find gaps in the tightest fields. Sobers was, of course, the perfect all-rounder. His strength as a batsman was that he could turn a match with awesome attacking shots. Both Pollock and Sobers were adventurous players and both were left-handed batsmen. Of the old timers, I would have to select **Jack Hobbs**, who was a textbook stylist. The most perfect post-war English batsman was without any doubt **Peter May**. He had a shot for every occasion.

MY IDEA OF THE PERFECT BOWLER

Ray Lindwall and **Keith Miller**, my old Australian adversaries, share the accolade. Both had beautiful actions to go with their natural flair, and were a perfect balance for each other. Ray was poetry in motion, with a Rolls Royce of a smooth action. His fastest ball could be unplayable. Keith used to blow hot and cold. He would deliberately lure the batsman into a sense of false security with slowish balls, and then suddenly unleash a thunderbolt. There has not been a better pairing in the history of Test cricket. **Freddie Trueman** and **Brian Statham** formed a great partnership for England, and for their first series against England **Ramadhin** and **Valentine** were close to perfection as spin twins. Of the modern players, **Lillee** and **Thomson** are in the Miller and Lindwall class, and young **Michael Holding** looks as fast as any bowler in history.

MY BEST BATTING PERFORMANCE

I have to choose my unbeaten knock for England against Australia at Old Trafford in 1948. I edged a ball from Ray Lindwall into my face and had to leave the field to have stitches inserted in a gash on my brow. I had scored just four runs and England were in trouble at 32 for two. I resumed my innings at 119 for five and managed to make an unbeaten 145. Keith Miller and Ray Lindwall were good mates of mine, but that did not stop them bowling bouncers at me when I came back in. It was all part and parcel of the competitive nature of Ashes cricket. Great fun.

MY BEST BOWLING PERFORMANCE

It can only be my five for 70 off 25 overs against South Africa at Cape Town in the 1948-9 third Test. I did not bowl any of my 'chinamen' or googlies, and just concentrated on left-arm orthodox leg breaks on a wicket conducive to spin. I managed to break a third-wicket stand of 190 between Dudley Nourse and Bruce Mitchell, and the other eight South African wickets then fell for just 58 runs. It was the only time in my Test career that I took five wickets. In that same series I was proud, surprised even, to bowl eleven maidens in a sixteen-over spell in the first Test in Durban.

BEST BATTING PERFORMANCE WITNESSED

There are so many that queue in my memory – a double century by Andrew Sandham when I was a wide-eyed youngster, 254 by the great Don Bradman at Lord's when I was a spectator at the Nursery End and Len Hutton's doggedly determined 364 while I was sitting in the Oval dressing-room waiting my turn to bat. But the innings I have to pick above all others is **Stan McCabe's** magnificent 232 for Australia against England at Trent Bridge in 1938. I caught him off Hedley Verity's bowling but not before he had severely punished our attack. My fingers stung for hours after catching him. Don Bradman called his Australian team-mates to the balcony and said, "Come and watch. You will never see better than this." And he was right.

MY FAVOURITE GROUNDS
Lord's, naturally, is my number one choice but I have three others very close to my heart for a variety of reasons: **Old Trafford**, **Trent Bridge**, and the **Oval**. Overseas, I have particularly fond memories of the **Adelaide Oval**, and any number of grounds in South Africa with **Newlands**, standing beneath Table Mountain, quite breathtakingly beautiful.

PLAYERS I MOST ADMIRE OUTSIDE MY SPORT
Golfer **Gary Player** is the sportsman I most admire. He was not born with the greatest natural talent for his game but achieved greatness through sheer dedication. Gary competed head to head with Arnold Palmer and Jack Nicklaus and often got the better of them at a time when golf was just beginning to boom as a major sport. Here in England **Henry Cotton** was a wonderful trend setter who made European golfers raise their standards. I always liked the way my good friend **Ted Woodward** played rugby for Wasps and England. He would tuck the ball under his arm and go hell for leather for the line. Great stuff to watch. **Lester Piggott** rivals even the great **Sir Gordon Richards** as the greatest jockey of all time, and in boxing I am sure there has never been an entertainer to match **Muhammad Ali**, although I was brought up in an era when gentleman **Joe Louis** was the king. If I am allowed to choose footballers,

I would pick **Alex James, Joe Mercer** and **Stanley Matthews** from my time in the game, and from recent years **Bobby Charlton, Denis Law, George Best, Jimmy Greaves** and **Bobby Moore**. Alex James was the finest controller of a game that I ever played with. He could dictate the pace with his passes, and he would put his foot on the ball and look imperiously around him to make an assessment of where he could next do the most damage. Joe Mercer was a born leader who could get the best out of the players around him with his driving captaincy, while Stanley Matthews was simply the best winger there has ever been - just ahead of the versatile **Tom Finney**. I have loved watching Charlton, Law and Best weave their magic for Manchester United, and Jimmy Greaves is the greatest poacher of goals I have ever seen. Bobby Moore was the most composed defender, who always seemed to have time and space in which to work even when under severe pressure.

THE TEAM I WOULD MOST LIKE TO CAPTAIN

I would have selected masters such as Sir Jack Hobbs. Patsy Hendren and Wilfred Rhodes, but I was restricted to making my choice from players who have featured in post-war Test cricket. Walter Hammond would have been another of my selections, but his peak years were before the war. My hardest task was having to leave out Ian Botham, who has been England's great find as an all-rounder. But I have decided on Garfield Sobers and Keith Miller as my all-rounders. They do not come better than this. Godfrey Evans just got the nod ahead of Rodney Marsh and Alan Knott for the wicket-keeper's role. The Don will be the captain, although I feel that Richie Benaud was probably a better tactician. Lillee and Lindwall will open the bowling. Fancy being able to toss the ball to Keith Miller as first-change bowler! If the wicket is taking spin, the multitalented Garfield Sobers can bowl his slow stuff in support of Richie Benaud and his magical leg spin. This would be my "unbeatable" team ...

Len Hutton (England)
Barry Richards (South Africa)
Don Bradman (Australia)
Viv Richards (West Indies)
Peter May (England)
Garfield Sobers (West Indies)
Keith Miller (Australia)
Richie Benaud (Australia)
Ray Lindwall (Australia)
Godfrey Evans (England)
Dennis Lillee (Australia)
12th man: **Sunil Gavaskar** (India)

Extras: The Scoreboard

*I was never one for paying too much
attention to statistics. I was happy
to leave others to do the counting.*
Denis Compton

Compo's Test match record,
innings by innings

The following statistical section has been compiled with constant reference
to the cricket bible, *Wisden Cricketers' Almanack*, and various collected works
by my old Fleet Street colleague Bill 'The Bearded Wonder' Frindall.

Test No 1 v New Zealand, Kennington Oval 1937
First innings: run out 65
Second innings: did not bat
Bowling: 6 overs 0 maidens 2 for 34
Match drawn
*Run out when the bowler deflected Joe Hardstaff's straight
drive on to the stumps. At 19 years and 84 days, Compo
was then England's youngest Test cricketer.*

Test No 2 v Australia, Trent Bridge 1938
First innings: c Badcock b Fleetwood-Smith 102
Second innings: did not bat
Match drawn
*At 20 years and 19 days, he was the youngest player ever to
score a century for England. Shared a record sixth wicket
stand of 206 in 138 minutes with Eddie Paynter (216 not out).*

Test No 3 v Australia, Lord's 1938
First innings: lbw b O'Reilly 6
Second innings: not out 76
Match drawn
Australian captain Don Bradman shook Compo's hand at the end of the match and said that his 76 not out was "a masterpiece of an innings".

Test No 4 v Australia, Headingley 1938
First innings: b O'Reilly 14
Second innings: c Barnett b O'Reilly 15
Australia won by five wickets

Test No 5 v Australia, Kennington Oval 1938
First innings: b Waite 1
Second innings: did not bat
England won by an innings and 579 runs
Len Hutton scored a then world record 364

Test No 6 v West Indies, Lord's 1939
First innings: c Stollmeyer b Cameron 120
Second innings: did not bat
Bowling: 3 overs 0 maidens 0 for 8
England won by eight wickets
Shared a whirlwind fourth wicket stand of 248 runs in 148 minutes with Hutton (196)

Test No 7 v West Indies, Old Trafford 1939
First innings: hit wicket b Clarke 4
Second innings: not out 34
Match drawn

Test No 8 v West Indies, Kennington Oval 1939
First innings: c Gomez b Martindale 21
Second innings: not out 10
Bowling: 5 overs 1 maiden 0 for 20.
Match drawn

Test No 9 v India, Lord's 1946
First innings: b Amarnath 0
Second innings: Did not bat
England won by ten wickets
Bowled first ball by Amarnath

Test No 10 v India, Old Trafford 1946
First innings: lbw b Amarnath 51
Second innings: not out 71
Bowling: 4 overs 0 maidens 0 for 18
            3 overs 1 maiden   0 for 5
Match drawn

Test No 11 v India, Kennington Oval 1946
First innings: not out 24
Second innings: did not bat
Bowling: 5 overs 0 maidens 0 for 15
Match drawn

Test No 12 v Australia, Brisbane 1946-7
First innings: lbw b Miller 17
Second innings: c Barnes b Toshack 15
Bowling: 6 overs 0 maidens 0 for 20
Australia won by an innings and 332 runs

Test No 13 v Australia, Sydney 1946-7
First innings: c Tallon b McCool 5
Second innings: c Bradman b Freer 54
Australia won by an innings and 33 runs

Test No14 v Australia, Melbourne 1946-7
First innings: lbw b Toshack 11
Second innings: run out 14
Match drawn

Test No 15 v Australia, Adelaide Oval 1946-7
First innings: c & b Lindwall 147
Second innings: not out 103
Bowling: 3 overs 0 maidens 0 for 12
Match drawn
Compo and Arthur Morris both scored hundreds in each innings. It is the only time opposing batsmen have done this in the same Test. Godfrey Evans went a record 97 minutes without scoring in a match-saving stand with Compo

Test No 16 v Australia, Sydney 1946-7
First innings: hit wicket b Lindwall 17
Second innings: c Miller b Toshack 76
Bowling: 1.2 overs 0 maidens 0 for 8
Australia won by five wickets

Test No 17: v New Zealand, Christchurch 1946-7
First innings: b Cowie 38
Second innings: did not bat
Match drawn

Test No 18: v South Africa, Trent Bridge 1947
First innings: c Mitchell b Tuckett 65
Second innings: c Mitchell b Mann 163
Bowling: 2 overs 1 maiden 0 for 6
       4 overs 0 maidens 0 for 14
Match drawn
Compo and skipper Norman Yardley (99) set a fifth-wicket record for the series with a stand of 237

Test No 19 v South Africa, Lord's 1947
First innings: c Rowan b Tuckett 208
Second innings: Did not bat
Bowling: 21 overs 11 maidens 2 for 32
       32 overs 10 maidens 2 for 46

England won by ten wickets
Shared a then world record 370-run third wicket partnership with Bill Edrich

Test No 20 v South Africa, Old Trafford 1947
First innings: c Tuckett b Dawson 115
Second innings: hit wicket b Mann 6
Bowling: 7 overs 1 maiden 0 for 27
           17 overs 2 maidens 1 for 58
England won by seven wickets
Compo and Edrich put on 228 runs together in 196 minutes.

Test No 21 v South Africa, Headingley 1947
First innings: c Mitchell b Mann 30
Second innings: Did not bat
Bowling: 4 overs 0 maidens 0 for 9
           2 overs 0 maidens 0 for 10
England won by ten wickets

Test No 22 v South Africa, Kennington Oval 1947
First innings: c Tuckett b Rowan 53
Second innings: c Nourse b Dawson 113
Bowling: 11 overs 4 maiden 0 for 31
           4 overs 0 maidens 0 for 30
Match drawn
Compo batted 105 minutes and hit 14 fours.

Test No 23 v Australia, Trent Bridge 1948
First innings: b Miller 19
Second innings: hit wicket b Miller 184
Bowling: 4 overs 0 maidens 0 for 24
Australia won by eight wickets
Compo took 410 minutes scoring his 184 in an innings spread over three days because of constant rain interruptions. He had to restart his innings ten times.

Test No 24 v Australia, Lord's 1948
First innings: c Miller b Johnston 53
Second innings: c Miller b Johnston 29
Bowling: 3 overs 0 maidens 0 for 11
Australia won by 409 runs

Test No 25 v Australia, Old Trafford 1948
First innings: not out 145
Second innings: c Miller b Toshack 0
Bowling: 9 overs 3 maidens 0 for 18
Match drawn
Hooked a bouncer from Lindwall into his face when four and retired hurt at 33 for two. Resumed his innings (a plaster covering a stitched wound on his forehead) after the fall of the fifth wicket, batted 327 minutes and hit 16 fours.

Test No 26 v Australia, Headingley 1948
First innings: c Saggers b Lindwall 23
Second innings: c Miller b Johnston 66
Bowling: 17 overs 6 maiden 2 for 38
          15 overs 3 maidens 1 for 82
Australia won by seven wickets

Test No 27 v Australia, Kennington Oval 1948
First innings: c Morris b Lindwall 4
Second innings: c Lindwall b Johnston 39
Bowling: 2 overs 0 maidens 0 for 6
Australia won by an innings and 149 runs

Test No 28 v South Africa, Durban 1948-49
First innings: c Wade b Mann 72
Second innings: b McCarthy 28
Bowling: 2 overs 0 maidens 0 for 5
          16 overs 11 maidens 1 for 11
England won by two wickets

Test No 29 v South Africa, Johannesburg 1948-9
First innings: c Mtchell b Mann 114
Second innings: did not bat
Bowling: 10 overs 0 maidens 1 for 34
　　　　　13 overs 3 maidens 0 for 31
Match drawn

Test No 30 v South Africa, Cape Town 1948-9
First innings: b Rowan 1
Second innings: not out 51
Bowling: 25.2 overs 3 maidens 5 for 70
　　　　　3 overs 1 maiden 0 for 7
Match drawn
Bowling orthodox left-arm leg breaks, Compo had a five wicket haul for the only time in his Test career.

Test No 31 v South Africa, Johannesburg 194-9
First innings: c A. Rowan b Tuckett 24
Second innings: b Markham 25
Bowling: 4 overs 0 maidens 0 for 19
　　　　　9 overs 2 maidens 0 for 35
Match drawn

Test No 32 v South Africa, Port Elizabeth 194-9
First innings: c Wade b Mann 49
Second innings: c Cheetham b A. Rowan 42
Bowling: 7 overs 0 maidens 0 for 39
　　　　　9 overs 0 maidens 0 for 57
England won by three wickets

Test No 33 v New Zealand, Headingley 1949
First innings: st Mooney b Burtt 114
Second innings: c Mooney b Cave 26
Bowling: 8 overs 2 maidens 1 for 23
　　　　　1 over 0 maidens 0 for 5
Match drawn

Test No 34 v New Zealand,Lord's 1949
First innings: c Sutcliffe b Burtt 116
Second innings: b Burtt 6
Bowling: 7 overs 0 maidens 1 for 33
Match drawn

Test No 35 v New Zealand,Old Trafford 1949
First innings: b Cowie 25
Second innings: did not bat
Bowling: 6 overs 0 maidens 1 for 28
        8 overs 0 maidens 1 for 28
Match drawn

Test No 36 v New Zealand, Kennington Oval 1949
First innings: c Scott b Cresswell 13
Second innings: did not bat
Bowling: 2 overs 0 maidens 1 for 6
        1 over   0 maidens 0 for 3
Match drawn

Test No 37 v West Indies, Kennington Oval 1950
First innings: run out 44
Second innings: c Weekes b Valentine 11
Bowling: 7 overs 2 maidens 0 for 21
West Indies won by an innings and 56 runs

Test No 38 v Australia, Brisbane 1950-1
First innings: c Lindwall b Johnston 3
Second innings: c Loxton b Johnston 0
Australia won by an innings and 70 runs

Test No 39 v Australia, Sydney 1950-1
First innings: b Miller 0
Second innings: c Johnson b Johnston 23
Bowling: 6 overs 1 maiden 0 for 14
Australia won by an innings and 13 runs

Test No 40 v Australia, Adelaide Oval 1950-1
First innings: c Tallon b Lindwall 5
Second innings: c sub. Loxton b Johnston 0
Bowling: 1 over 0 maiden 0 for 11
       4.6 overs 1 maiden 1 for 18
Australia won by 274 runs

Test No 41 v Australia, Melbourne 1950-1
First innings: c Miller b Lindwall 11
Second innings: not out 11
England won by eight wickets

Test No 42 v New Zealand, Christchurch 1950-1
First innings: b Burtt 79
Second innings: did not bat
Bowling: 4 overs 0 maidens 0 for 21
       2 overs 0 maidens 0 for 10
Match drawn

Test No 43 v New Zealand, Wellington 1950-1
First innings: b Burtt 10
Second innings: b Cresswell 18
England won by six wickets

Test No 44 v South Africa, Trent Bridge 1951
First innings: c Waite b McCarthy 112
Second innings: lbw b Mann 5
Bowling: 2 overs 0 maidens 0 for 7
       2 overs 0 maidens 0 for 10
South Africa won by 71 runs

Test No 45 v South Africa, Lord's 1951
First innings: lbw b McCarthy 79
Second innings: did not bat
Bowling: 2 overs 0 maidens 0 for 13
England won by ten wickets

Test No 46 v South Africa, Headingley 1951
First innings: lbw b A. Rowan 25
Second innings: lbw b Mann 5
Bowling: 1 over 0 maidens 0 for 4
       7 overs 1 maiden 0 for 16
Match drawn

Test No 47 v South Africa, Kennington Oval 1951
First innings: b McCarthy 73
Second innings: c Van Ryneveld b Chubb 18
Bowling: 1 over 0 maidens 0 for 5
England won by four wickets

Test No 48 v India, Headingley 1952
First innings: c Ramchand b Ghulam Ahmed 14
Second innings: not out 35
Bowling: 7 overs 1 maiden 0 for 20
England won by seven wickets

Test No 49 v India, Lord's 1952
First innings: lbw b Hazare 6
Second innings: not out 4
Bowling: 7 overs 0 maidens 0 for 10
England won by eight wickets

Test No 50 v Australia, Trent Bridge 1953
First innings: c Morris b Lindwall 0
Second innings: did not bat
Match drawn

Test No 51 v Australia, Lord's 1953
First innings: c Hole b Benaud 57
Second innings: lbw b Johnston 33
Match drawn

Test No 52 v Australia, Old Trafford 1953
First innings: c Langley b Archer 45
Second innings: did not bat
Match drawn

Test No 53 v Australia, Headingley 1953
First innings: c Davidson b Lindwall 0
Second innings: lbw b Lindwall 61
Match drawn

Test No 54 v Australia, Kennington Oval 1953
First innings: c Langley b Lindwall 16
Second innings: not out 22
England won by eight wickets
Compo hit a boundary to clinch the regaining of the Ashes.

Test No 55 v West Indies, Jamaica 1953-4
First innings: lbw b Valentine 12
Second innings: b Ramadhin 2
Bowling: 2 overs 1 maiden 0 for 5
       1 over 0 maiden 0 for 13
West Indies won by 140 runs

Test No 56 v West Indies, British Guiana 1953-4
First innings:c Stollmeyer b Atkinson 64
Second innings: did not bat
Bowling: 3 overs 1 maiden 0 for 6
England won by nne wickets

Test No 57 v West Indies, Trinidad 1953-4
First innings: c & b Ramadhin 133
Second innings: did not bat
Bowling: 8.4 overs 1 maiden 2 for 40
       7 overs 0 maiden 0 for 51
Match drawn

Test No 58 v West Indies, Barbados 1953-4
First innings: c King b Valentine 13
Second innings: lbw b Stollmeyer 93
Bowling: 5 overs 0 maiden 0 for 29
West Indies won by 181 runs

Test No 59 v West Indies, Jamaica 1953-4
First innings: hit wicket b King 31
Second innings: did not bat
Bowling: 13 overs 2 maidens 1 for 36
Match drawn

Test No 60 v Pakistan, Lord's 1954
First innings: b Fazal 0
Second innings: did not bat
Bowling: 2 overs 1 maiden 0 for 5
Match drawn

Test No 61 v Pakistan,Trent Bridge 1954
First innings: b Khalid 278
Second innings: did not bat
England won by an innings and 129 runs
*The highest Test innings of Compo's career included a six
and 33 fours. He shared a fifth wicket stand with Trevor Bailey
during which they put on 192 runs in 105 minutes.*

Test No 62 v Pakistan, Old Trafford 1954
First innings: c Imtiaz b Shujauddin 93
Second innings: did not bat
Match drawn

Test No 63 v Pakistan, Kennington Oval 1954
First innings: c Imtiaz b Fazal 53
Second innings: c Imtiaz b Fazal 29
Pakistan won by 24 runs

Test No 64 v Australia, Brisbane 1954-5
First innings: not out 2
Second innings: c Langley b Benaud 0
Australia won by an innings and 154 runs
Compo batted last in each innings after fracturing a bone in his left hand when he ran into a fence while fielding.

Test No 65 v Australia, Melbourne 1954-5
First innings: c Harvey b Miller 4
Second innings: c Maddocks b Archer 23
England won by 128 runs

Test No 66 v Australia, Adelaide Oval 1954-5
First innings: lbw b Miller 44
Second innings: not out 34
England won by five wickets

Test No 67 v Australia, Sydney 1954-5
First innings: c & b Johnson 84
Second innings: did not bat
Match drawn

Test No 68 v South Africa, Trent Bridge 1955
First innings: lbw b Adcock 27
Second innings: did not bat
England won by an innings and 5 runs

Test No 69 v South Africa, Lord's 1955
First innings: c Keith b Heine 20
Second innings: c Mansell b Goddard 69
England won by 71 runs

Test No 70 v South Africa, Old Trafford 1955
First innings: c Waite b Adcock 158
Second innings: c Mansell b Heine 71
South Africa won by three wickets

Test No 71 v South Africa, Headingley 1955
First innings: c Mansell b Tayfield 61
Second innings: c Waite b Goddard 26
South Africa won by 224 runs

Test No 72 v South Africa, Kennington Oval 1955
First innings: c Waite b Goddard 30
Second innings: c Waite b Fuller 30
England won by an innings and 92 runs

Test No 73 v Australia, Kennington Oval 1956
First innings: c Davidson b Archer 94
Second innings: not out 35
Match drawn

Test No 74 v South Africa, Johannesburg 1956-7
First innings: c Keith b Goddard 5
Second innings: c & b Tayfield 32
England won by an innings and 131 runs

Test No 75 v South Africa, Cape Town 1956-7
First innings: c McLean b Tayfield 58
Second innings: c & b Goddard 64
Bowling: 2 overs 1 maiden 0 for 3
England won by 312 runs

Test No 76 v South Africa, Durban 1956-7
First innings: b Heine 16
Second innings: c Keith b Tayfeld 19
Bowling: 1 over 0 maiden 0 for 5
Match drawn

Test No 77 v South Africa, Johannesburg 1956-7
First innings:c Pithey b Heine 42
Second innings: c Goddard b Tayfield 1
South Africa won by 17 runs

Test No 78 v South Africa, Port Elizabeth 1956-7
First innings: b Adcock 0
Second innings: c Endean b Tayfield 5
South Africa won by 58 runs

Breakdown

Batting:
131 innings 15 not out 5807 runs 17 hundreds 28 fifties
Average: 50.06
Highest score: 278 (v Pakistan, Trent Bridge 1954)
Bowling:
2716 balls 1410 runs 25 wickets Average: 56.40

Best analysis: 5 for 70 (v South Africa, Cape Town 1948-9)

Test catches held: 49

Compo's Test match scores, country by country:

	Innings	No! out	Runs	l00s	50s	Highest	Average
Australia	51	8	1,842	5	9	184	42.83
South Africa	42	1	2,205	7	11	208	53.78
West Indies	14	2	592	2	2	133	49.33
New Zealand	11	0	510	2	2	116	46.36
India	8	4	205	–	2	71*	51.25
Pakistan	5	0	453	1	2	278	90.60

Compo scored 3,963 of his runs (av. 60.04) in home Tests, and 1,844 (av. 36.88) while on tours.

Extras: Compo chronology

1918: 23 May, born at 47 Alexandra Road, Hendon, Middlesex. Father, Harry, was a self-employed carpenter and decorator. His mother, Jessie, was a former housemaid. He had a six years older brother, Leslie, and an older sister, Hilda, who were both born in Woodford, Essex.

1923–32: Attended Bell Lane Elementary school where he became captain of both the cricket and football teams. Played representative football and cricket for Hendon and Middlesex schools, and played in England schoolboy football trials. Selected as twelfth man for England schoolboy football internationals against Scotland and Wales.

1931: Scored 114 at Lord's Nursery ground when skippering the London Elementary schools team against the Public Schools. Invited to join the Middlesex and Arsenal groundstaffs.

1932: Left school at fourteen at Easter to work at Lord's in the summer and at Highbury in the winter. Coached at Lord's by first George Fenner and then Archie Fowler. Ordered to wear a slipper on his left foot while training at Arsenal in a bid to get him to make more use of his right foot.

1935: Wearing boots, bat and whites borrowed from 6 foot 3 inch wicket-keeper George Brown, out for a first-ball duck in his MCC debut against Suffolk at Felixstowe. Scored 110 in the second innings after being reunited with his own kit that he had left behind at Lord's. Played his first match with Bill Edrich. They went in at number ten and eleven for MCC against Beaumont College.

1936: County debut for Middlesex against Sussex at Lord's in May 1936 seven days past his eighteenth birthday. Scored his maiden first-class century against Northants after coming in at number eight, and became the youngest player to score 1,000 runs in his first season. Made his League debut for Arsenal against Derby County in a 2–2 draw at Highbury on 26 September. It was the first of just fifty-four League matches that he played for Arsenal over the next fourteen years.

1937: Made his Test debut against New Zealand at the Oval on 14 August. Run out for sixty-five. At 19 years and 84 days, he was the youngest England Test debutant. Totalled 1,980 runs at an average 47.14.

1938: Scored his first Test century (102) against Australia at Trent Bridge in June at the age of 20 years and 19 days. Shared a record fifth-wicket partnership of 206 with Eddie Paynter. Totalled 1,868 runs at an average 45.56. Had a cartilage operation on his right knee following a collision with the Charlton Athletic goalkeeper.

1939: Averaged 63 in five Tests against the West Indies, with a top score of 120. Totalled 2,468 runs at an average 56.09. Became a Special Constable on the outbreak of war in September.

1940-5: War service as a physical training instructor and weapons trainer. Played fourteen wartime internationals for England as an outside left, with Stanley Matthews on the right wing and Tommy Lawton leading the attack. Scored seventy-four goals in 126 wartime matches for Arsenal, helping them win the Regional League three times and playing a creative role in a 7-1 crushing of Charlton Athletic in the Football League South Cup Final at Wembley in 1943. Posted to India as a sergeant-major, he played seventeen first-class cricket matches. They included a game for Holkar in March 1945 in the final of the Ranji Trophy against Bombay. A then world record 2,078 runs were scored. He made 249 not out in the second innings. Started a lifelong friendship with Keith Miller in India where he was playing for an Australian Services XI.

1946: After an uncertain start to the first post-war season, Compton led the batting averages with 2,403 runs at an average of 61.61. Was about to switch from the orthodox left-arm slow bowling to the leg spin (including a googly and 'chinaman') to which he was introduced by Leicester's Australian spinner Jack Walsh. Scored 146 runs at an average 73.00 in two Tests against India. On his first overseas tour (1946-7 to Australia) he scored 459 Test runs at an average 51.00. In the Adelaide Oval Test he scored a century in each innings (147 and 103 not out). Scored thirty-eight runs in his one Test innings in New Zealand.

1947: The golden summer. Compton accumulated 3,816 runs, the highest aggregate in a season of first-class cricket anywhere in the world. He topped the averages with 90.85, and scored a record 1,187 runs against the South African tourists, including six centuries. His Test average against the tourists was 94.12, with a highest score of 208. The 2,048 runs he scored at Lord's is the highest aggregate on one ground in a season. His eighteen first-class centuries beat by two the record set by his hero Sir Jack Hobbs in 1925. He became the first English batsman to score 1,000 Test runs in a calendar year (1,159 at an average 82.78). The thirteen centuries he scored in the County Championship remains the Middlesex record. He also took seventy-three wickets with his leg spin. His "twin" Bill Edrich scored 3,539 runs (average 80.43 and including twelve centuries) and took sixty-seven wickets. Together they shared six stands of more than 200: 370 for England v South Africa at Lord's; 287 against Surrey; 277 against Leicestershire; 228 for England against South Africa at Old Trafford; 223 against Sussex; and 211 against Northants. It was not just a two-man show by Middlesex. Openers Jack Robertson (2,760) and Syd Brown (2,078) also plundered plenty of runs as Middlesex raced to the County Championship.

1948: Compton (252 not out) and Edrich (168 not out) shared an unbroken stand of 424 for Middlesex against Somerset at Lord's, which remains the highest third-wicket partnership by an English team in England, the highest Middlesex partnership for any wicket, and the highest for any wicket against Somerset. The summer Test series belonged to Don Bradman's Australian tourists, but Compton still managed a healthy collection of 562 Test runs at an average 62.44. On 3–4 December 1948, playing for MCC against North-eastern Transvaal at Benoni, Compton scored the fastest triple century on record, scorching to 300 in 181 minutes. He and Reg Simpson (130 not out) put on 399 for the third wicket (a South African record). Compton scored 198 of his runs in boundaries (5 sixes, 42 fours). His first 100 took 66 minutes, his second 78 minutes and he raced to his third century in just 37 minutes. Collected a League championship winner's medal for his fourteen First Division appearances with Arsenal.

1949: After scoring 1,781 runs on the 1948–9 tour of South Africa (average 84.80), Compton helped himself to 2,530 runs at home (average 48.65). He scored 300 of the runs in six Test innings against New Zealand at an average 50.00.

1950: His FA Cup winner's medal for Arsenal against Liverpool at Wembley in 1950 was a golden climax to his football career. Standing 5 foot 11 inches tall, his weight had gone to around 14 stone and he was no longer fit enough for the challenge of First Division football. A floating bone in his right kneecap was giving him problems and his Test match appearances against the West Indies were restricted to just two innings in which he scored fifty-five runs. His curtailed season produced 957 runs at an average 45.57.

1951: He had the most dismal Test series of his career in Australia on the 1950-1 tour when he was vice-captain to Freddie Brown. Scored just fifty-three runs in eight Test innings at an average 7.57, and added 107 runs in two Tests in New Zealand (average 35.66). He found flashes of his old form against his favourite opponents South Africa in the summer series in England, scoring 312 in six Test innings at an average 52.00. His total haul was 2,193 runs at an average 64.50.

1952: The Knee was continuing to handicap him, and he scored a total of "only" 1,880 runs at an average 39.16 between hospital treatment. In four Test knocks against India he scored 59 runs at an average 29.50.

1953: Always remembered as the year in which England regained the Ashes, and Compton scored the series-clinching winning runs with a boundary in the Oval Test. He scored 234 runs in eight Test innings at an average 33.42. His aggregate for the season was 1,659 runs at an average 39.50. On the 1953-4 tour to West Indies he totalled 630 Test runs at an average 39.50.

1954: Produced his highest Test score and the highest by any batsman at Trent Bridge with 278 against Pakistan. He amassed 273 of his runs in one day, a total only twice previously surpassed by Don Bradman and Walter Hammond. His 192-run partership with Trevor Bailey was a fifth-wicket record against Pakistan. Scored a total 1,524 runs at an average 58.61. In the 1954-5 Test series in Australia he scored 191 runs at an average 38.20.

1955: South Africa brought almost the best out of him again despite his knee handicap, and he scored 492 Test runs at an average 54.66. His total for the season was 1,209 runs at an average 34.54. But his knee had now become locked and the decision was made to remove the kneecap.

1956: Made a memorable comeback in the final Test against Australia, scoring 94 in what Sir Donald Bradman described as the finest innings of the series. His total runs for an abbreviated season was 705 at an average 35.25.

1957: After scoring 242 Test runs at an average 24.20 on the 1956-7 South African tour, the limping Compton decided to bow out of Test cricket and have just one more season chasing runs with Middlesex. He totalled 1,554 runs at an average 34.53, including a century in his final match for Middlesex against Worcestershire at Lord's in August 1957.

Cricket career summary: Compo accumulated 38,942 runs in his first-class career (839 innings), at an average 51.85. He scored 123 centuries, his century of centuries coming in just 552 innings, a feat surpassed only by Bradrnan (295 innings). His career record:

839 innings 88 not outs 38,942 runs 123 100s 183 50s Highest score 300. Career average: 51.85

As a bowler, he took 622 wickets at an average 32.27, and he held 415 catches.

1958–: Continued to play exhibition and guest-match cricket until 1964, particularly with the Cavaliers. Started a career as a broadcaster (BBC Television), cricket columnist and football reporter *(Sunday Express)* and working as a consultant to McCann Ericson in the advertising world. Married his Christine in 1972, and they had tweo daughters, Charlotte and Victoria. From two previous marriages, Denis had three sons, Brian, Patrick and Richard.

1997: Denis passed away on St George's Day, 23 April, aged 78.

J.J. (John) Warr, former President of the MCC and once Compo's Middlesex team-mate, had the Westminster Abbey congregation rocking with laughter during his moving and amusing address when he said: "Compo took 415 catches, that was when he was looking ...!" It was a reference to Compo's tendency to allow his concentration to wander when the batting ever became boring.

Compo was never boring.

Extras: The Storytellers

All of us acknowledge the skills that Denis was
given and which he so flamboyantly employed. We
celebrate the pleasure that he gave.
Dr Wesley Carr

IT would have been an impossible task for me to gather the Compo stories on my own, and I have many people to thank for helping in the compilation. I have been lucky during my journalistic career to have had as colleagues cricket writing masters E.M. (Lyn) Wellings, the legendary Charles Bray (with whom I worked on the *Daily Herald*) and my esteemed team-mate from the *Daily Express* days, Crawford White. I used to drain all of them of their Compo stories, without consciously realising that I would one day pull together their memories to help me compile a celebration of Compo's life and times.

They reported in an era when they used to protect as well as project the players. "I feel sorry for the modern players in the way they come under the media microscope," Compo told me. "They would have had a field day with us with that sort of intrusive reporting, but we could trust the press in my day and, more often than not, they were at our side exercising their elbows at some pretty riotous parties."

Clearly, many of the Compo stories will never be told.

I am indebted to doyen of freelance sports reporters Dennis Signy for allowing me, while editor of the *Hendon Times*, access to the prewar files; also to my old friend Peter Watson for passing on his notes from the 1977 Centenary Test trip to Melbourne when most surviving England Test cricketers were in the tour party and had a Compo story to tell.

The library staff at the *Sydney Morning Herald* were both patient and pleasant (considering I was a Pom) when I called in to raid their archives, and Stephen Green, the Lord's librarian, is to be congratulated on the way he keeps the Compton collection in pristine condition at cricket's headquarters. My former *This Is Your Life* colleagues, and in particular Sue Green and Tom Wettengel, were a great source of information and inspiration.

The entire Compton family, led by Christine, were friendly and forthcoming with stories on the night that Compo was the pleasantly surprised recipient of the Red Book from Eamonn Andrews, who was a main motivator in making me dig for the untold stories.

I have continually cross-checked for facts with the bible of cricket, *Wisden Cricketers' Almanack*, and have also leaned heavily on those excellent magazines *Wisden Cricket Monthly* and *The Cricketer*; also any number of statistical collations by my old Fleet Street colleague Bill "The Bearded Wonder" Frindall. The Press Association and Popperfoto kindly provided the photographs, and Don Macpherson designed the stunning jacket.

Most of all my thanks to publisher Tim Forrester of André Deutsch/Chameleon Books for encouraging me to see the project through, mainly because of his own schoolboy hero worship of Compo. Thanks, too, to Louise Dixon for her editing skills, and Michael Giller for his statistical input.

Here, chapter by chapter, are the storytellers who helped put the punchlines into my Compo collection.

Chapter 1, Farewell Compo
(1) J.J. (John) Warr, Westminster Abbey address, and various author and agency interviews with: (2) Keith Miller; (3) John Major; (4) Peter O'Toole; (5) Lord Cowdrey; (6) Dr Wesley Carr, Dean of Westminster, (7) Lord Runcie of Cuddenson, (8) E.W. (Jim) Swanton; (9) Dennis Skinner; (10) Sir Alec Bedser, (11) Sir Tim Rice; (12) Jimmy Tarbuck; (13) Fred Titmus; (14) Mike Gatting; (15) Godfrey Evans; (16) Peter Hill-Wood; (17) Lord Archer; (18) Ted Dexter; (19) Tom Graveney; (20) Mrs. Christine Compton; (21) Richard Compton.

Chapter 2, The First Runs

(1) Denis Compton, various author's interviews; (2) Mark Mitchell, London *Evening Star* 1931; (3) Harry Compton, London *Evening News* 1947; (4) Leslie Compton, various author's interviews; (5) Arthur McIntyre, London *Evening News* 1955; (6) Sir Pelham Warner, London *Evening News* 1955; (7) Hilda Addington (Denis's sister), author's *This Is Your Life* notes; (8) Mrs Jessie Compton, Denis's mother, London *Evening News* 1947; (9) Lord's coach George Fenner, London *Evening News* 1947; (10) Lord's coach Archie Fowler, author's interview 1968 for *Daily Express* Sports Forum column; (11) Patsy Hendren, London *Evening News* 1955.

Chapter 3, Out for a Penny

(1) Denis Compton, various author's interviews; (2) Sir G.O. (Gubby) Allen, author's *This Is Your Life* notes; (3) Maurice Tate, London *Evening News* 1947; (4) Harold Larwood, author's interview 1969 for *Daily Express* Sports Forum column; (5) R.W.V. (Walter) Robins, author's interview for *Daily Herald* 1963; (6) Ian Peebles, author's interview 1970 for *Daily Express* Sports Forum column; (7) Jim Sims, London *Evening News* 1955.

Chapter 4, Taking the Test

(1) Denis Compton, various author's interviews; (2) Harry Compton, *Hendon Times* 1937; (3) R.W.V. (Walter) Robins, author's interview for *Daily Herald* 1963; (4) Lord's coach Archie Fowler, author's interview 1968 for *Daily Express* Sports Forum column; (5) Joe Hardstaff, author's interview 1969 for *Daily Express* Sports Forum column; (6) Bill O'Reilly, Centenary Test notes and the files of the *Sydney Morning Telegraph*.

Chapter 5, Hutton: the Truth

(1) Sir Leonard Hutton, author's *This Is Your Life* notes; (2) Denis Compton, various author's interviews; (3) Film actor

Trevor Howard, author's interview for *Book of Cricket Heroes* 1984.

Chapter 6, The Footballer
(1) Denis Compton, various author's interviews; (2) Leslie Compton, various author's interviews; (3) Ted Drake, author's interview 1990; (4) Laurie Scott, DCSC obituary interview, 1997; (5) Tommy Lawton, author's interview 1987; (6) Joe Hulme, author's interview, 1972; (7) Bernard Joy, author's interview with the London *Evening Standard* football correspondent 1971; (8) Eddie Hapgood, author's interview for *Daily Express* Sports Forum column 1972; (9) Bill Shankly, author's interview 1969; (10) Joe Mercer, author's interview 1987.

Chapter 7, Compo at War
(1) Leslie Compton, various author's interviews; (2) Denis Compton, various author's interviews; (3) Benny Green, author's *This Is Your Life* notes; (4) Sir Stanley Matthews, author's interview 1997; (5) Stan Cullis, author's interview 1987; (6) Bernard Joy, author's interview with the London *Evening Standard* football correspondent 1971; (7) Wilf Mannion, author's interview for *Daily Express* Sports Forum column 1969; (8) General Zia ur Rahman, author's *This Is Your Life* notes; (9) Reg Simpson, author's interview 1980.

Chapter 8, Golden Nugget
(1) Denis Compton, various author's interviews; (2) Keith Miller, various author's interviews.

Chapter 9, The Terrible Twins
(1) Denis Compton, various author's interviews; (2) Bill Edrich, various author's interviews.

Chapter 10, The Summer of '47
(1) Denis Compton, various author's interviews; (2) Bill

Edrich, various author's interviews; (3) Sir Jack Hobbs, London *Evening News* 1947; (4) Lord's coach Archie Fowler, 1947; (5) Doug Insole, author's *This Is Your Life* notes; (6) Tom Goddard, London *Evening News* 1955; (7) Alan Melville, London *Evening Star*, 1947; (8) O.C. (Ossie) Dawson, DCSC obituary notes; (9) Godfrey Evans, author's *This Is Your Life* notes; (10) Doug Wright, London *Evening News* 1947; (11) Neville Cardus, the *Guardian*.

Chapter 11, The Compton Knee
(1) Denis Compton, various author's interviews; (2) Bill Edrich, various author's interviews; (3) Sir Leonard Hutton, author's *This Is Your Life* notes; (4) Peter May, author's *This Is Your Life* notes; (5) Osmond Clarke, London *Evening News* 1955; (6) Sir Jack Hobbs, London *Evening News* 1955.

Chapter 12, Butcher of Benoni
(1) Reg Hayter, various author's interviews; (2) Jimmy Greaves, various author's interviews; (3) Reg Simpson, author's interview 1980; (4) John Arlott, author's *This Is Your Life* notes; (5) Peter Watson, various author's interviews; (6) Bill Edrich, various author's interviews.

Chapter 13, Black-eye Drama
(1) Denis Compton, various author's interviews; (2) Sir Donald Bradman, the files of the *Sydney Morning Telegraph*; (3) Godfrey Evans, author's *This Is Your Life* notes; (4) Bill Edrich, various author's interviews; (5) Keith Miller, various author's interviews (6).

Chapter 14, The Final Runs
(1) Denis Compton, author's interviews; (2) Sir Len Hutton, author's *This Is Your Life* notes; (3) Keith Miller, various author's interviews; (4) Neil Harvey, D.C.S.C. obituary notes; (5) Peter May, author's *This Is Your Life* notes; (6) Bill Edrich, author's interviews; (7) Martin Horton, *Evening News* 1957.

Chapter 15, Brylcreem Boy
(1) Reg Hayter, various author's interviews; (2) Frank Nicklin, various author's interviews; (3) Bagenal Harvey, author's interview; (4) John Shrewsbury, author's interview 1997; (5) Peter Watson, various author's interviews; (6) Denis Compton, various author's interviews; (7) Peter O'Sullevan, author's interview.

Chapter 16, A Marrying Man
(1) Denis Compton, various author's interviews; (2) Eamonn Andrews, author's interview 1987; (3) Brian Compton; (4) Sir G.O. (Gubby) Allen, (5) Ted Woodward, (6) Ted Dexter, (7) Colin Milburn, (8) Godfrey Evans, (9) Joe Mercer, (10) Sir Alec Bedser, (11) J.J. (John) Warr, (12) Trevor Bailey, (13) Fred Trueman, (14) Doug Insole, (15) Colin Ingleby-Mackenzie, (16) Keith Miller ... all author's *This Is Your Life* notes.

Chapter 17, Tales of the Unexpected
(1) Peter Parfitt, author's *This Is Your Life* notes (Peter was unavailable to appear on the show but is the acknowledged Denis Compton expert); (2) Fred Titmus, author's interview for *Daily Express* Sports Forum 1970; (3) RWV (Walter) Robins, London *Evening News* 1955; (4) PGH Fender, Centenary Test notes; (5) Eddie Paynter, Centenary Test notes; (6) Jack Young, *This Is Your Life* notes; (7) Lindsay Hassett, author's interview 1981; (8) Godfrey Evans, author's *This Is Your Life* notes; (9) Colin Bland, D.C.S.C. obituary notes; (10) Maurice Tremlett, London *Evening News* 1955; (11) Cyril Washbrook, London *Evening News* 1955; (12) Sir Garfield Sobers, author's interview for *Daily Express* Sports Forum 1972; (13) Rachel Heyhoe-Flint, D.C.S.C. obituary notes; (14 and 19) Bill Edrich, various author's interviews; (15) Brian Statham, DCSC obituary notes; (16) Rt Rev. David Sheppard, Bishop of Liverpool, author's interview for *Daily Express* Sports Forum 1968; (17) Alan Oakman, author's *This Is Your*

Life notes; (18) Jack Crapp, author's interview 1977; (20) Tommy Trinder, author's interview for *Daily Express* Sports Forum; (21) Tom Graveney, various author's interviews; (22) Leslie Compton, various author's interviews; (23) Norman Yardley, London *Evening News* 1957; (24 and 28) Paul Gibb, Centenary Test notes; (25) Eric Bedser, London *Evening News* 1955; (26) Harry Potts, author's interview; (27) Joe Mercer, author's *This Is Your Life* notes; (29) Jimmy Greaves, author's interview; (29) Dickie Bird, D.C.S.C. obituary notes; (30) Roy Ullyett, author's interview; (31) Frank Tyson, Centenary Test notes; (32) Wayne Larkins, author's interview; (33) Terry Lawless, author's interview 1997; (34) Ted Woodward, author's *This Is Your Life* notes; (35) Reg Gutteridge, author's interview; (36) Sir Malcolm Sargent, author's interview, Saints and Sinners dinner, 1966; (37) Bobby Moore, author's interview, Saints and Sinners dinner, 1966.

Extras: The Thanksgivers

Thanks to the kind cooperation of Stephen Holmes, Assistant Receiver General at Westminister Abbey, I am able to give the following line-up of family, dignitaries and Compo admirers who attended the Thanksgiving Service for the Life of Denis Compton CBE on 1 July 1997. This was the release from the Abbey:

A Service of Thanksgiving for the life of Mr Denis Compton cricketer and footballer, was held in Westminster Abbey at noon on Tuesday 1 July 1997. The Dean of Westminster, the Rev Dr Wesley Carr, officiated assisted by the Precentor, the Rev Barry Fenton. Mr Peter Hill Wood, Chairman, Arsenal Football Club, and Mr Richard Compton read the lessons and Mr E.W. Swanton read Lord's from *English Cricket* by Neville Cardus. Mr John James Warr gave an address.

The Rt Rev Lord Runcie said prayers. Canon David Hutt and the Rev Jonathan Goodall, Chaplain and Sacrist, were robed and in the Sacrarium. Among others in the large congregation were:

Family:
Mrs Christine Compton (widow)
Brian Compton, Patrick Compton, Richard Compton (sons)
Charlotte Compton, Victoria Compton (daughters)
Mrs Richard Compton (daughter-in-law)
Mr Nicholas Compton

Miss Alexandra Compton
Mr and Mrs Alan Compton
Mr Freddie Compton
Miss Isobel Compton
Mrs Hilda Addington (sister)
Mr and Mrs Ray Gorhan,
Mr and Mrs Lionel Johnson
Mr Adam Lane
Mrs Betty Lovelace
Mr and Mrs Ian Mooney
Mr and Mrs Sidney Windsor
Mrs Jennifer Yeatman,
Mrs A. Hilton.
Dignitaries:
Lord MacLaurin of Knebworth, Chairman, English and
Welsh Cricket Board, with Mr Tim Lamb, Chief Executive
Lord Archer of Weston-super-Mare
Lord Cowdrey, President of the Lord's Taverners
Lord Griffiths,
Lord Howie of Troon
Lord Kingsland QC
Lord (Brian) Rix
Lord Vestey
John Major, MP
Sir Peter Emery, MP
Sir Nicholas Scott
The Hon Mervyn Greenway
The Hon Sir Clive Bossom
The Hon Neil MacLaurin
Sir Scott Baker
Sir Alec Bedser and Eric Bedser
Mr and Mrs Keith Miller
Sir Hugh Bidwell
Sir William Doughty
Sir Paul Fox, representing the BBC
Sir Donald Gosling

Sir Anthony Grant
Sir Michael Marshall
Lady (George) Martin
Sir Leslie and Lady Murphy
Mr Justice Popplewell
Sir Tim Rice
Lady Riches,
Sir Denis Rooke
Sir Stanley Simmons
Sir Anthony Tuke
Sir Peter Yarranton.
Mr Colin Ingleby-Mackenzie, President, MCC, and Mrs Ingleby-Mackenzie
Mr Mike Murray, President, Middlesex CCC, with Mr Alan Moss, Chairman, and Mr Joe Hardstaff, Secretary, and the full Middlesex playing and groundstaff
Mr Peter Hill-Wood and Mr Ken Friar, Arsenal FC
Mr Paul Sheldon, Chief Executive Surrey CCC
Mr M.F. Hill, President, Somerset County Cricket Club
Mr Peter Edwards, Secretary, Essex County Cricket Club
Mr Hugh Griffiths, Secretary Sussex County Cricket Club
Mr A.J. Holton, Chairman, Northamptonshire CCC
Mr David Richards, Chief Executive, International CC
Mr Patrick Shervington, Director the Lord's Taverners and Mr John Bromley, Chairman
Mr P.A. Snow, Fiji Cricket Association.
Mr Eric Budd, Honorary Secretary, The Cricket Society
Mr M. Furse, President, Club Cricket Conference
M. J.O. Trumper, President, Incogniti Cricket Club
Mr Donald Bruce, Secretary, Cricketers Club of London
Mr Martin Hardy, Express Newspapers
Mr Stephen Lynch, *Wisden Cricket Monthly*
Mr Neil Benson, Secretary, Saints and Sinners Club
Mr D. Warden, Chairman, McCann Ericson Advertising
Mr P. Brown, The Forty Club
Mrs Elsa Davies, National Playing Fields Association

241

Mr Peter Nathan, London Playing Fields Society
Mr K. Borrett, Berks, Bucks & Oxon Union of Golf Clubs
Ms Shulpa Patel, BBC Radio *Test Match Special*

*Others present at Westminster Abbey on July 1 1997 giving
thanks for the life of Denis Compton included:*

Allen, Mr Patrick
Amiss, Mr Dennis
Arnoldi, Mr and Mrs H.W.
Astaire, Mr Jarvis
Baird, Dr M.A.
Baker, Dr B.
Banks, Mrs G.E.
Barclay, Mr John
Barnes, Mr John
Barratt, Mr Michael
Barrett, Air Commodore F.O.
Bates, Mr Terry
Bennett, Mr Don
Bidwell, Mr Julian
Bird, Squadron Leader J.K.
Blofeld, Mr Henry
Booth, Mr and Mrs Roy
Bourdillon, Mr and Mrs P.I.
Bowen, Mr James
Brewer, Mr Geoffrey
Brocklehurst, Mr and Mrs B.
Brooker, Mr A.B.
Brooke-Taylor, Mr and Mrs Tim
Brotherton, Mr M.L.
Brown, Canon Simon
Brown, Mr and Mrs Bill
Brown, Mr Keith
Brown, Mr Tony
Browne, Dr D.
Bunker, Mr A.R.

Burshnell, Dr Mark
Butlin, Mr R.F.
Carlisle, Mr John
Carr, Mr and Mrs Donald
Carr, Mr John
Carr, Mrs Wesley
Carson, Mr Mike
Clark, Mr D.G.
Close, Mr R.E.
Coker, Mr Paul
Coldwell, Mr and Mrs L.S.
Cole, Mr John
Coleman, Mr B.
Cook, Mr Jimmy
Coral, Mr Bernard
Corrigan, Mr T.S.
Cox, Mr Barry
Crabbe, Mr Michael
Craig, Dr David
Crompton, Mr Alan
Crowder, The Ven N.H.
Cundy-Cooper, Mrs E.
Cuthbertson, Mr Colin
Darby, Dr David J.
Davidson, Mr and Mrs Alan
Davies, Mr Alan
Davies, Mr Dickie
Dawson, Mr Miles
De Sousa, Mr Gerald
Dean, Mr B.G.

Dean, Mr D.S.
Dean, Mrs G.M.
Delisle, Mr. Peter
Denison, Mr Michael and
Miss Dulcie Gray
Dexter, Mr and Mrs Ted
Dickson, Dr D.H.W.
Doble, Mr D.H.
Dodds, Mr T.C.
Downing, Mr Brian
Dowson, Mr Graham
Durden-Smith, Mr Neil and
Ms Judith Chalmers
Earl, Miss Karen
Edmonds, Mr and Mrs Phil
Elder, Dr and Mrs M
Eldridge, Mr A.J.
Emmerson, Mr J.C.
Empson, Mr John
Endersbee, Mr B.J.
Evans, Mr David
Evans, Mr Godfrey
Eves, Mr David
Fairbairn, Mr Alan
Finney, Mr Albert
Fletcher, Mr Keith
Fowler, Mr M.H.
Fox, Mr H.M.
Francis, Mr T.
Fraser, Mr Angus
Freedman, Mr Louis
Freer, Mr George
Frewin, Mr Michael
Frith, Mr and Mrs D.W.
Fry, Mr C.A.
Gakhar, Mr David
Gakhar, Mr Raj

Gale, Mr and Mrs Bob
Gallimore, Mr W.A.
Gatting, Mr and Mrs Bill
Gatting, Mr and Mrs Mike
Giller, Mr Norman
Godfray, Mr D.J.L.
Godfrey, Mr Alan
Gosling, Mr F.J.
Gould, Mr Ian
Grace, Mr Graham
Grainger, Mr Eric
Graveney, Mr and Mrs Tom
Graveney, Mr Tim
Gray, Mr and Mrs Andrew
Green, Mr Benny
Green, Mr Michael
Green, Mr Richard
Greenway, Mr Harry
Greenwood, Mr John
Greenwood, Mr Peter
Guyver, Mr C.
Hadingham, Mr R.E.H.
Hardie, Prof. and Mrs J.M.
Harding, Mr and Mrs Derrick
Harris, Mr J.F.
Harris, Mr R.D.
Harwood, Robert
Harwood, Ronald
Havergal, Col Malcolm
Heald, Mr Brian
Heald, Mr Tim
Heard, Mr P.G.
Hely-Hutchinson, Mr Henry
Herbert, Mr F.W.
Heyhoe-Flint, Ms Rachel
Hilton, Mr and Mrs Derek
Hitchcock, Mr Clive

Hobbs, Mr M.F.
Hobbs, Mr Robin
Holland, Mr David
Holmes, Mr and Mrs Stanley
Holmes, Mr G.M.
Holmes, Mr Peter
Howard, Mr and Mrs W.B.
Howard, Mr C.G.
Hudson, Mr Robert
Hutchinson, Mr and Mrs A.
Hyman, Mr Robin
Ingleby-Mackenzie, Miss A.
Insole, Mr Douglas
Ireland, Mr A.W.V.
Jackson, Mr and Mrs T.
Jayston, Mr Michael
Jenkins, Mr J.C.
Jenkins, Mr Vivian
Johnson, Miss Jane
Johnson, Mr D.W.F.
Johnson, Mr Richard
Johnson, Mr Roger
Johnson, Mrs Sue
Judd, Mrs J.E.
Kallis, Mr Jacques
Kelly, Mr Llam
Killick, Miss Anne
Kilmartin, Mr John
Kindersley, Mr Guy
Kindersley, Mrs M.
King, Mr D.E.
Knight, Mr and Mrs Roger
Knudsen, Dr Anthony
Kolbert, His Hon Dr Colin
Kosminsky, Mr Leon
Lander, Mr Chris .
Lawrence, Mr J.W.

Lewis, Mr Vic
Lloyd, Mrs M.
Lotbiniere, Mr Henry de
Lowe, Mr Chris
Lucas, Dr and Mrs E.G.
Lucas, Mr George
Major, Mr William
Makin, Mr Chris
Mann, Mr Brian
Mann, Mr George
Marchant, Mr and Mrs D.J.
Marlar, Mr Robin
Marsh, Mrs R.J.
Martin-Jenkins, Mr Christopher
May, Mrs Peter
MacCaskill, Mr and Mrs Iain
McBride, Commandant V.A.
McCarthy, Dr Brian
McDonald, Mr and Mrs Colin
Meagher, Rev Thomas
Medwin, Mr Michael
Melford, Mr M.A
Mence, Mr Michael
Michelmore, Mr Cliff
Millar, Mr and Mrs J.S.
Mirzoeff, Mr Edward
Morgan, Mr Cliff
Neary, Mrs Martin
Neligan, Mr and Mrs T.
Nicholas, Mr Mark
Nicklin, Mr Frank
O'Brien, Mr Ray
O'Toole, Mr Peter
Palmer, Mr Charles
Parker Bowles, Mr Simon
Parkhouse, Dr R.M.E.
Parry-Jones, Mr David

Paul Getty II, Mr and Mrs J.
Pemberton, Mr and Mrs O.
Pigott, Mr and Mrs W.D.
Pocock, Mr Pat
Pooley, Mr Jason
Potts, Rev G.A.
Powell, Mr Robert
Price, Mr J.A.
Raman Subba Row, Mr and Mrs
Ramprakash, Mr Mark
Redfern, Mr and Mrs Derek
Redmond, Mr P.J.
Redpath, Rev George
Reeder, Mr Jim
Reeder, Mr. A.R.
Reeve, Mr James
Regan, Dr N.A.
Richards, Mr David
Richards, Mr W.S.C.
Roberton, Dr J.C.
Roberts, Mr A.E.
Robins, Mr Charles
Robins, Mr R.V.C.
Rogers, Canon K.
Ross, Mr Alan
Rouse, Mr W.J.C.
Rowe, Mr C.A.
Royds, Mr Nicholas
Ruoff, Mr Harold
Russell, Mr C.J.M.
Russell, Mr Eric
Ryall, Mr C.
Sanders, Mr Peter
Sangster, Mr Robert
Schofield, Mr Ken
Scovell, Mr Brian
Seth-Smith, Mr A.

Shackleton, Mr J.A.P.
Silverstone, Dr Brian
Sissons, Mr Michael
Skeffington, Mr Neville
Skinner MP, Mr Dennis
Smale, Mrs Louise
Smith, Mr Alan
Smith, Mr Brian
Smith, Mr J.H.
Smith, Mr Mike
Snow, Mr V.J.
Snow, Rear-Adml Kenneth
Stacpoole, Mr Robert de
Statham, Mr Brian
Steel, Mr D.M.A.
Stephenson, Lt-Colonel J.R.
Stewart, Mr and Mrs Micky
Sturt, Mr Mike
Summers, Mr D.C.
Surridge, Mrs Betty
Swanton, Dr and Mrs A.R.
Swanton, Mrs E.W.
Tarbuck, Mr Jimmy
Tarlin, Mr Derek
Taylor, Mr Brian
Tewson, Miss Josephine
Thomas, Mr Leslie
Tierney, Mr Kieran
Timberlake, Mr C.A.
Titmus, Mr Fred T
Trueman, Mr A.D
Tufnell, Mr Phil
Ufton, Mr and Mrs Derek
Upton, Mr Alan
Vine, Mr and Mrs B.J.
Walker-Arnott, Mr J.S.
Warr, Mrs J.J.

Watkins, Mr Alan
Weaver, Mr L.J.
Webster, Mr David
Weekes, Mr Paul
West, Mr Peter
Weston, Mr G.W.
Wheatley, Mr and Mrs Ossie
Whitcombe, Mr P.A.
Williams, Dr David
Williams, Mr Colin

Williams, Mr Gerald
Williams, Mr J.M.
Wilson, Mr and Mrs Don
Wilson, Mr Lynn
Woodcock, Mr H.E.P.
Woodcock, Mr John
Woodhouse, Mr and Mrs A.J.P.
Wooldridge, Mr and Mrs Ian
Wyndham, Mr Henry

There were many more friends and colleagues from the worlds of cricket, football, advertising and the media, as well as hundreds of unnamed people who just wanted to be there to give their thanks for the life of the one and only Denis Compton.

And we all had our own Compo stories to tell.

INDEX